try and make me!

try and make me!

Simple Strategies That Turn Off the Tantrums and Create Cooperation

Ray Levy, Ph.D., and Bill O'Hanlon, M.S., L.M.F.T.
with Tyler Norris Goode

RODALE

REACH™

Notice

This book is intended as a reference v̶̶̶̶̶̶̶̶̶̶̶̶̶̶̶̶̶̶̶̶̶̶̶̶̶̶̶̶̶̶̶ ̶̶̶̶̶̶̶̶̶̶̶nanual. The information given here is designed to help you make informed decisions about your child's behavior. It is not intended as a substitute for any treatment that may have been prescribed by your psychologist or doctor. If you suspect that your child has medical or psychological problems, we urge you to seek competent professional help.

© 2001 by Ray Levy, Bill O'Hanlon, and Tyler Norris Goode
Illustration © by Karen Kuchar

Printed in the United States of America
Rodale Inc. makes every effort to use acid-free ∞, recycled paper ♻

The chart on page 11 is reproduced from David McClelland, *Human Motivation* (New York: Cambridge University Press, 1988). Reprinted with permission.
The chart on page 26 is reproduced from Russell A. Barkley, *Defiant Children: Parent-Teacher Assignments* (New York: Guilford Press, 1987). Reprinted with the permission of Guilford Press.
The technique Attending to Play is based on Russell A. Barkley, *Defiant Children: Parent-Teacher Assignments* (New York: Guilford Press, 1987).

Jacket art direction: Richard Kershner
Jacket photograph © JBF/Stone

Library of Congress Cataloging-in-Publication Data

Levy, Ray.
    Try and make me! : simple strategies that turn off the tantrums and create cooperation / by Ray Levy and Bill O'Hanlon with Tyler Norris Goode.
        p.   cm.
    Includes index.
    ISBN 1–57954–335–9 hardcover
    1. Child rearing. 2. Child development. 3. Temper tantrums in children.
4. Communication in the family. 5. Children—Conduct of life. 6. Attitude change in children. I. O'Hanlon, William Hudson. II. Goode, Tyler Norris.
III. Title.
HQ769 .L399 2001
649'.1—dc21   00–011042

Distributed to the book trade by St. Martin's Press
2 4 6 8 10 9 7 5 3 1   hardcover

RODALE

WE **INSPIRE** AND **ENABLE** PEOPLE TO IMPROVE
THEIR LIVES AND THE WORLD AROUND THEM

Dr. Ray Levy

To Nancy and Laurie, who showed me what loving and dedicated
parenting can do, and for pushing me when I wanted to give up

To Susan, Rachel, and Abbey, who make coming
home every day truly rewarding

Bill O'Hanlon

To Steffanie, who never makes me do anything
but has changed me greatly through her loving manner

And to Patrick, Zachary, Nick, and Angie, my children
and stepchildren, who have taught me a lot about how
and how not to parent

Tyler Norris Goode

To Wende: Magic happens all around you—
thanks for making me a part of it

To Mom and Dad: For committing your lives to
raising Allen and me right

To "Coach" and Bill: For this opportunity and your friendship

To God: For making it all possible

Contents

Part You Solve It, or I'll Solve It . . . and You Won't Like My Solution

Resources

Index

Acknowledgments

In September 1995, Dr. Ray Levy and Bill O'Hanlon sat down to tape-record their preliminary thoughts on the subject of how to raise a strong-willed child. A few months later, Ray enlisted the help of Tyler Norris Goode to help turn their ideas into a book.

Over the next 2 years, Ray—a perfectionist at heart—decided that he and Tyler would reorganize, rehash, and ultimately rewrite most of *Try and Make Me!* until a suitable publisher could be found. The writing of this book reached its climax when Bill convinced his two coauthors to join him at his home in Santa Fe, New Mexico, for a long weekend of intense work on the book. The synergy between the three coauthors surprised them all, and those 3 days transformed this project into a labor of fun as Bill, Ray, and Bill's wife, Steffanie, kept the mood light from sunup until sundown. The result, we think you'll find, is that the approach in this book is warm—and even comical in places.

The three coauthors would like to thank their better halves for their assistance in this project. Susan Porter-Levy, Steffanie O'Hanlon, and Wende Goode filtered through raw text for more than 100 hours each and offered suggestions for improvements. (Each of these women has extensive experience in dealing with strong-willed kids as social workers and therapists.) They also waited patiently while we husbands spent hour after hour trying to make this book flow better.

Ray would like to thank Joe Cates for coming up with the concepts of Academies and the four types of consequences, and for his help in developing both. More important, he appreciates the gifts of

Joe's friendship and encouragement, which have been priceless the last few years.

Ray would also like to thank his nephew Bram, whose defiant antics entertained him for hours, drove Bram's mother crazy, and gave Ray material for this book.

Dr. Jim Harrison was instrumental in helping Ray see that strong-willed children don't respond to negativity in the manner that many other children do.

Finally, Ray would like to thank Bill for his friendship, leadership, and humor, and "Coach" for his friendship, sheer persistence, and wonderful ability to write and "Tylerize."

The authors would also like to express their appreciation to Rodale in general and Kevin Ireland specifically for injecting a positive dose of energy into this project.

Ray and Tyler would like to thank Bill and Steffanie for opening up their home that weekend in Santa Fe.

Thanks also to Lynn Spurgin for the role she played in helping Tyler find out about this project.

The coauthors appreciate the following "guinea pigs" who read a rough draft of *Try and Make Me!* and offered their suggestions and comments: Pam Bell; Pat McKay; Martha Queen; Susan Martin, Ph.D.; and the lady who sat next to Ray on an American Airlines flight from Iowa.

Introduction

*E*very year, through our practices and the hundred-some workshops and seminars that we each give, we meet dozens of parents and other adults. And often they voice the same concern: Their troublesome kids are driving them up the wall.

Sound familiar? It's not surprising. Many adults today are tearing their hair out with anger and frustration from dealing with defiant, oppositional, or strong-willed kids. No matter how hard these adults try, no matter how much they love these kids, they just can't seem to help their kids learn to cooperate and behave. Our message to them is the same one we share with you: Don't give up. There is help.

It's in the principles that we explain in this book.

Within these pages, you'll find a program of progressive steps you can use to curb your child's defiance and encourage compliance. You'll discover why your kids act the way they do in your home, classroom, or counselor's office. You'll learn why other methods you may have tried didn't work and, in fact, may have made the situation worse. Then, in the last three sections, you'll find some very logical, practical, and simple techniques you can use to turn your defiant child into the more loving, well-behaved youngster you're probably dreaming about right now.

Allow us to be frank: Making things better will take some amount of time, energy, and—most of all—love on your end. But if you follow the nonmedical strategies that we suggest, they will work. We've seen it happen in case after case, whether we're helping a concerned couple, a single parent, or a teacher, social worker, minister, or school counselor who works closely with a defiant child and knows that something must change in his life for him to get better.

Even parents of generally good kids—ones who rarely get out of line—can benefit by following the strategies we explain in *Try and Make Me!*

Defiant kids usually come in two varieties: They are born or made. Some kids are just going through a phase of life or an emotionally trying time, and they act out by being defiant every time they don't get their way. Other kids are defiant from the moment they come into the world kicking and screaming. They have a genetic predisposition to being defiant and headstrong. They may have attention deficit hyperactivity disorder (ADHD) or other neurological problems that lead to—or add to—their problems. Beyond these basic types of defiant kids, there's a third group: those who bend the rules only occasionally, but sure know how to turn your ears red whenever they do.

All these kids can be taught how to behave better. In fact, they usually want to behave better. They really do desire a good relationship with the adults in their lives. They also want structure and discipline, but they lack the behavior skills to get there on their own.

This book will help you build those skills. We can practically guarantee it.

In our more than 50 years of combined experience, we have not seen a single child who could not be helped using the strategies outlined in this book. If you follow the advice we offer, it will improve your relationship with your child, it will reduce your child's defiance, and it will help your child develop or enhance the skills he needs to be friendly, cooperative, and socially well-adjusted.

Some Quick Explanations

A few notes on language before we get started. The first is that we primarily use the term *defiant* throughout this book when referring to children who are oppositional, strong-willed, or just plain difficult. Specialists make technical distinctions among these terms. But we think that if you are dealing with one of these kids in your family, in the classroom, or in the therapy room, you'll know what we mean. We figure that you are less interested in technical distinctions than in getting some practical help.

Second, when we're talking about our advice or our collective opinion on a matter, we use the terms *we* and *us*. When referring to a specific case that one of us has encountered, we talk about "Ray's case" or "Bill's client."

Third, we use the term *he* when we are not referring to a specific child but to the generic "defiant child." We do this primarily because it makes our book easier to read than if we had sprinkled "he or she" or "they" all through the text. (Another reason for using "he" generically is that most of these kids are boys, even though girls can be defiant as well, of course.)

Fourth, we use a few borderline-vulgar terms that kids commonly spout, even though they are distasteful, to let you know that we understand that you hear these terms—and worse—from the kids you deal with. (Hope we don't offend you.)

Throughout *Try and Make Me!* we offer examples from our own lives and families as well as from our therapy practices. When we use stories from our practices, we have changed the names to protect confidentiality. Some details in those stories have also been changed to ensure that people won't be recognized from the descriptions here.

Finally, to avoid awkwardness in phrasing and to create a more seamless writing flow, we speak with one voice even though this work is a collective effort between psychologist and child therapist Ray Levy and family therapist Bill O'Hanlon (along with our writing partner, Tyler Norris Goode).

One Final Note

This book is designed to be a practical, useful guide for caring parents, teachers, and others who want to help defiant children overcome their problems. If you have issues that make it difficult for you to control your temper, or if you struggle with a history of abusing children, this book is *not* designed to help you. Nor will it help if your defiant child is abusing drugs. In these cases, seek assistance directly from a licensed therapist.

But aside from those situations, we believe that this book can improve your relationship with your sometimes tough-to-love child.

Part

1

Why Did Our House Turn Into a War Zone?

Okay. Maybe your home or classroom isn't *technically* a war zone. But you have to admit that it feels that way sometimes, doesn't it? When your child puts his beans in his ears at the dinner table . . . when your student superglues every computer mouse in your classroom to a desk . . . when your kid just won't listen and keeps acting up, he is disrupting the peace. And that, by definition, is a war.

This first part will give you some insight into why your child puts his hands on his hips, smirks at you, and says, "Try and make me!" Once you have a clear understanding of why he is the way he is, you'll be better equipped to do battle and reclaim some of the peace that's been missing in your life.

Winning the Brat War

We May Have to Lie in the Beds We Make, but That Doesn't Mean That We Can't Change the Sheets

*E*ric Cranberry was turning his mother's hair a premature gray.

Each morning, she would gently rub his head and sweetly urge him to get out of bed. Eric's response? "Leave me alone! Get out of my room." Or he'd grunt to let her know that she wasn't wanted.

A weary Mrs. Cranberry would exit her son's room and dejectedly walk downstairs to the kitchen, hoping that somehow Eric would rouse himself and get ready for school.

It seemed like years since Eric had behaved like a rational youngster. Instead, every word from his lips now seemed designed to tear his mother up, and Mrs. Cranberry was running out of the will to deal with his rotten attitude. Somehow, though, she still managed to put on a cheery face 5 minutes later when she returned to his bedroom and tried to prod the second grader out of bed again.

Eric finally got out of bed, but the morning ritual resumed when he found his way to the breakfast table, looked at what was on his plate, and uttered his familiar demand: "I don't want eggs. Give me Captain Crunch!" Rather than escalate the battle, Mrs. Cranberry quietly caved in so that her son would hurry up and get ready for school. She sighed as she poured the kiddie cereal, and she sighed again minutes later when he sat at the edge of his bed, hands folded, unwilling to put on the clothes they'd picked out together the night before.

Sweet Mrs. Cranberry tried coaxing him into dressing. She pulled his shirt over his head when he refused to do it himself, then patiently tied his shoes when he balked at that too. Then, she combed the tangled web of hair on his head so he wouldn't look ridiculous and drove him to school.

After battles like this, she always needed several cups of soothing herbal tea and an hour of silence to recover.

Finally, she decided that she had to change the situation, so she made an appointment with a psychologist—which is how Ray Levy met her. Every day was a nightmare, she explained to Ray, and she begged for some solution. For his part, Eric sat on the other side of the office, doing his best to act bored. Midway through the first session, he unloaded with "This is stupid!"

Observing what a little terror the Cranberrys had on their hands, Ray suggested that Mrs. Cranberry drop in for a visit the next day while young Eric was occupied at school.

Ray and Mrs. Cranberry mapped out a plan during that next session—a plan aimed at motivating Eric by holding him accountable for his behavior. Mrs. Cranberry was reluctant to try the strategy at first, out of fear that her son might end up missing breakfast, which she'd heard is the most important meal of the day. Ray assured her that Eric would live, and do fine in school, even if he missed a meal. Reassured, Mrs. Cranberry put the plan in motion.

That night, Eric was momentarily caught off guard when his mother handed him an alarm clock and rattled off the new expectations.

"So you just need to set the alarm right here for whatever time you want to get up," Mrs. Cranberry explained. "Breakfast will be served between 7:00 and 7:20, and my car leaves the house at 7:40." With that, she left the room and took a deep breath, hoping for the best.

At 7:20 the next morning, Mrs. Cranberry sat alone in the kitchen. It was all she could do to sit still and not wake her young son. Minutes crept by until, finally, at 7:30, the youngster came down the stairs demanding, "I want my breakfast! Why didn't you wake me up?"

Mrs. Cranberry managed to say, "Breakfast was only from 7:00 until 7:20. It's too late now. Better hurry, though, because my car leaves in 10 minutes."

Of course, 7:40 came and went with Eric sitting defiantly in the same position at the breakfast table. Mrs. Cranberry inhaled deeply again and escorted her boy toward the garage (still in his Ninja Turtle pajama bottoms). Picking up a bag of clothes she'd packed the night before, she loaded Eric and all the baggage into her car.

Once inside the car, Eric hopped into the backseat. As Mom drove the two blocks to school, he kicked the back of her seat incessantly. She didn't complain; she just drove while bouncing back and forth with her son's kicks.

When they arrived at school, Eric bellowed, "I'm not going to school like this; try and make me!" And with that, a game of cat-and-mouse ensued. Mrs. Cranberry would open one back door and try to get Eric, but he'd back away. She'd then run to the other side of the car, open a door there, and Eric would elude her again. Finally, after 5 minutes of this, Mom buckled and drove the boy home to let him dress.

Angry, she called Ray to say that she was ready for a refund—the plan had failed miserably.

Ray wasn't ready to give in just yet, though. He made a phone call to the principal at Eric Cranberry's elementary school and asked for a little cooperation. He then called Mrs. Cranberry back and told her to give the plan one more try the next morning—and this time, she was to honk her horn if Eric refused to get out of the car.

The next day, the same routine unfolded, all the way up to Eric kicking his mother's seat on the ride to school. When they pulled up to the school and his mother told him that it was time to get out, Eric again piped up, "Try and make me!"

Rather than playing his little game, Mom Cranberry replied, "I don't have to." Instead, she lay on her horn.

Eric's eyes grew wide as his principal, Mr. Gathright, made his way from the front office to Mom's Nissan.

"Hello, Eric," Mr. Gathright said as he opened the back door. "Come with me."

Defenseless with fright, Eric waddled into school, clad only in his Ninja Turtle pajama britches and carrying the grocery bag of clothes. About to enter school, his second-grade friends watched and pointed. "That's not fair!" were the last words that Mom heard out of Eric's mouth as he headed into school.

Mr. Gathright called Ray later that morning to say that he'd never seen a youngster dress so quickly.

In the weeks, months, and years that followed, Eric caused other problems and got into other trouble. But the ruckus he stirred up never rivaled that battle of going to school his second-grade year.

Never, Ever Give Up

In that brief, 2-day episode, Mrs. Cranberry was able to use several of the principles from this book to put an end to the behavior that had been driving her senseless for almost 2 years. The actual methods that Mrs. Cranberry used will be explained in detail in the chapters that follow. But for now, the most important thing to remember from the Cranberry case is this: Never, *ever* give up on changing your strong-willed child's behavior.

No matter how miserable your child makes your life, no matter how hopeless your situation may seem on any given day, you can make a dramatic change in his attitude if you hang in there and apply the advice in this book. You may not see the immediate change that Mrs. Cranberry did, but don't be discouraged. The wonderful thing about working with kids who keep misbehaving is that you always get a second chance if things don't work out the first time.

It would have been easy for Mrs. Cranberry to accept defeat after she failed to get Eric out of the car that first day. She could have home-schooled him or moved him to a private school, or just lived with his rotten attitude. But the problem would still have been there. Instead, Mrs. Cranberry stuck with it for her son's sake and for her own sake. She used her second chance to do something different. And it paid off.

Where Defiance Starts

Four Reasons You Get Locked in Power Struggles with Your Child

One McDonald's television advertisement begins with a young boy teasing his mother's Persian kitty by dangling a stuffed mouse on a string. Every time the Persian pounces toward the bait, the boy yanks his fake rodent out of reach. Fed up, the agitated puss runs off to a local fast-food restaurant and purchases some bait of its own. The next thing we see is a large order of golden, steaming McDonald's fries drifting just above that same youngster's face. As the little tyrant hungrily bounds toward his favorite snack, the cat pulls it away. Poetic justice is served.

We know why the cat—and then the boy—leapt around like a bunny on steroids. Both wanted to satisfy their hunger. But the ultimate question that we adults ponder after watching that comedy routine is this: Why didn't the youngster allow the cat to play with its toy in the first place?

The answer is one word that we must always keep in mind when dealing with defiant children: *control*. It is the first of four characteristics that define defiant children.

A Deep Need for Control

Beyond the basics of love and attention that everyone craves, all kids are primarily motivated to reach one of three goals: achievement, friendship, or control. (See "What Makes Us Do the Things We Do?" on page 11.)

Kids motivated by *achievement* are the ones often considered high achievers or perfectionists by their parents and teachers. Picture the cat dangling a trophy or a high grade in front of these kids' faces. If there is a book contest, they want to read the most books. They play soccer because they want to score the most goals. These are the kids who go so far as to finish their weekend homework on Friday.

Children of this type are rarely referred for psychological treatment. When they do come to psychologists, they usually need help with stress because they have expected too much of themselves and have wound up with stomachaches.

Next are kids motivated by *friendship*, the desire to spend time with friends. To entice these kids, the cat would likely tease them with a telephone, instant messaging on the Internet, or overnights with friends. What these kids like most about school is recess and being with their friends. They play soccer not just for the love of the sport but for the love of hanging out with their buddies.

Children like this tend to be fairly easy to discipline. All you need to do is ground them or surgically remove the phones from their ears. We see a few kids like this in our practices, but not an extraordinary number. And most parents don't bother to buy books like this one when they have kids like those.

Finally come the kids who make up the majority of our workload, the ones you are probably dealing with if you are reading this book: children motivated by *control*. These are defiant children, for the most part, who size up the world by deciding what they can and cannot control. Even when they are toddlers, their whole purpose in stacking blocks is to knock the stack down.

One summer, on the beach, Ray was making a sand castle with his then-7-year-old defiant nephew, Bram. As Ray retrieved more water to help pack down sand on the yet-unfinished but expansive castle, he saw Bram jumping spread-eagled onto the architecture. In an instant, their construction was destroyed. Ray was annoyed, as almost any other adult would be (therapists aren't superhuman). But he later realized that, to Bram, the whole purpose of building a castle was to have the power to knock it down.

These kids enjoy things that they can control. Toys such as video games are popular with them. But although they enjoy gunning down the bad guys on a TV screen, they get much more satisfaction out of firing verbal barrages that cause you to explode in real life.

It's not a malicious thing at all, though it may seem that way. This is merely how these children learn to understand their lives and the world. They try to figure out what is and what is not within their reach. They like to keep the toy mouse away from the cat, and they enjoy controlling the cat's responses.

These kids are generally viewed as hard-headed or strong-willed. Obviously, these kids also have some achievement and friendship needs—as all children do—but the defiant kids want to gain or regain control more than anything else in the world.

The Desire to Manipulate Situations

A clever 8-year-old, Tad has attention deficit hyperactivity disorder (ADHD), is defiant, and is the product of a marriage that concluded in a nasty divorce. The parents often badmouth each other in front of Tad—so much so that Bill O'Hanlon, their counselor, has been forced to talk with them about it.

The reason that badmouthing was a problem became clear one day when Tad's mother picked him up at his father's house. Tad got into the car and demanded that his mother buy him a pricey Dallas Cowboys jacket. Mom calmly pointed out that he already had a very nice jacket and, in her judgment, did not need another. This led to a small temper

What Makes Us Do the Things We Do?

People are either motivated by a desired experience/goal or repulsed by an unpleasant/unwanted experience.

Motivated by

Money
Food
Better Health
Possessions
Sex
Status
Joy
Hunger

Repulsed by

Pain
Boredom
Harm/Danger

Children are primarily motivated by one of three goals:

Motivated by

Achievement
Affiliation/Friendships
Control

Defiant children are primarily motivated by one thing: control.

tantrum, which quickly—and surprisingly—ended. The young boy was quiet until they arrived at Mom's home. Then, Tad mumbled under his breath, "Dad was right. You do spend all the child-support money on yourself!" and slammed the car door.

Mom instantly got upset because she believed that Dad had once again been criticizing her in front of the youngster. She called Bill immediately to tell the whole story and to tattle on her ex-husband.

At his next therapy session with Tad, Bill grinned at Tad and asked, "Did Dad really say that, or did you make that up?"

He responded with a huge grin. "I made it up."

"Did it work?" the counselor asked.

"Yep!"

Tad demonstrated a behavior we call "socially perceptive and exploitive." He craftily took a social situation and manipulated it to his advantage.

Children like this are quite perceptive, and they can read a social situation from 100 yards away—just as Tad did. They will make subtle remarks or comments in order to stir things up because it is fun to them and it makes them feel powerful. For example, a defiant kid may provoke an uppercut from an older brother just so he can see his sibling get severely scolded.

Later in life, this ability to read how others will act can be a good thing. But as a child, someone who is socially exploitive only uses this skill to exploit and cause headaches for you.

Blind to Their Role in a Problem

Very often, defiant kids cannot see what role they play in creating problems. Instead, they mistakenly perceive themselves as victims. Many times, they even convince themselves that someone else is at fault.

One child Ray worked with several years ago exemplifies this trait, which psychologists have termed *cognitive misattribution*. School had let out early one winter day, and many children ran out into the parking to start a good-natured snowball fight. Ray's little patient was one of the last students out the door, and he stood right in the middle of the parking lot trying to figure out what all the commotion was about. As could be expected, a snow-sphere soon smacked him upside the head. Ray's client immediately ran over to the boy who had thrown the snowball, and he swatted his schoolmate's face several times.

When Ray asked the child a few days later about his behavior, he responded, "That boy threw the snowball at me on purpose. He was trying to make me look stupid."

Ray's little client was pinning a tail on the wrong donkey. Not only did this youngster not see his part in the problem (standing directly between two groups of students as they rifled clumps of snow at one another) but he also convinced himself that his classmate had it out for him.

Negativity Lovers

We've found another attribute that distinguishes these children: They can usually tolerate a lot of negativity.

During a power struggle, these kids thrive on levels of negativity and conflict that most adults can't tolerate. Defiant children almost literally eat and digest a monstrous argument within minutes. In other words, they have a high tolerance for struggles. Often, the conflict itself is rewarding to such children.

This is fascinating because it goes against one of the most basic ways in which people function. We humans, as a general rule, don't like anger. We don't like people to be angry with us. That's why many kids will comply when parents discipline them with angry emotions—like growling at the kids, squinting their eyes, changing the tone of their voice, and talking to them roughly.

But defiant kids tend to tolerate anger and emotional punishment very well. They may get upset, but they usually blow it off within minutes.

Dozens of parents have told us about times when they yelled, screamed, and practically pulled their own hair out scolding a defiant child. In all these instances, the child would go away to his room once the angry tirade subsided. Moments later, the child would come back out and ask for some favor, such as a Slurpee from the local 7-Eleven.

Still holding a grudge from all the yelling and screaming, the mother or father usually would think that the child was trying to be manipulative. But the truth—best as we can tell—is that the child had completely recovered from the yelling and screaming. We say that these children "consume negativity with their cornflakes." In fact, they don't even need milk to help wash down the conflict.

This final characteristic of defiant kids has an enormous impact

BEHAVIOR BASICS

Four Characteristics of Defiant Children

1. *Control-craving.* More than other kids, they crave control of their lives. They will do just about anything, even things that seem to produce the opposite result, to try to get, maintain, or regain control.
2. *Socially exploitive.* They are usually very quick to notice how others respond and to use those responses to their advantage in both social and family environments.
3. *Blind to their role in a problem.* Not only can they not see how they're affecting the problem, they convince themselves that people around them actually cause the problem intentionally.
4. *Able to tolerate a great deal of negativity.* They actually seem to thrive on large amounts of conflict, anger, and negativity from others. They'll win most times in escalating battles of negativity.

   Note: Beyond these characteristics, there is another difficulty that can make your child *seem* defiant: inflexibility. The inflexible child lacks sufficient behavior skills to handle any changes in his routines. You may think the child is misbehaving as a way to get under your skin, but the truth is he simply doesn't know how to react properly to anything with which he's not familiar.

on parenting and dealing with these children since we often use anger or negativity as a discipline tool. Increased negativity actually tends to enhance these kids' defiance rather than lessen it. Like a sponge soaking up water, they tend to feel larger and more powerful with every negativity meal. We will discuss ways to work around this obstacle later.

Stuck in a Rigid Pose: The "Inflexible Child"

If none of the characteristics we've listed above describe your child, he may well be what we call an "inflexible child."

All the children we've been talking about so far have the skills to behave but aren't motivated to use those skills. Inflexible children simply lack behavior skills. They don't know how to act appropriately in many situations, and the tiniest change can make them anxious or explosive.

Inflexible children desperately want things to be the same because routine provides them with safety, predictability, control, and—most important—freedom from anxiety. They also have trouble seeing how one situation is similar to another. For example, they often do not understand that cussing at a teacher is just as disrespectful as flipping her the bird and why they end up getting punished for both.

These children have another common characteristic: They often don't appear to learn from consequences. Being put into Time Out again and again has little or no effect on these children; after being released from Time Out, they often engage in the same behavior that got them into trouble in the first place.

To you and me, these kids appear defiant, strong-willed, explosive, or just plain hard-headed.

Consider Tad, an inflexible child who threw a major temper tantrum in his mother's minivan because Mom stopped for gas instead of going directly home from school as she usually did. Too inflexible to tolerate this seemingly insignificant change in routine, this 7-year-old blew a gasket, demanding that his mother "take me the hell home!"

Initially, his mother thought Tad didn't understand why the minivan needed gas, so she valiantly tried to explain the laws of automobile physics to him. When that failed to calm him, she again drew the wrong conclusion—this time thinking his behavior was controlling and manipulative. So she found herself locked in a power struggle with him, a conflict that further inflamed the boy's mood.

At that point in his anxiety, Tad simply was not capable of handling a change in plans, nor was he able to calm himself down.

Most 7-year-olds have the capacity to talk themselves through changes in routine without losing their cool. But inflexible children, who appear bright and intellectually capable in many areas, don't have the coping skills they need for handling even minor emotionally charged situations. They have great difficulty shifting gears. For instance, they may find it extremely hard to settle down after recess or lunch. Transition times tend to be difficult and stressful for them and are the occasions when they wreak the most havoc.

If kids like Tad are upset or already having a bad day, then any little change or request can send them over the edge. And to further frustrate the adults in their lives, these kids rarely feel ashamed of their behavior—something that most children would naturally experience. Worse, when an inflexible child grows emotional, he drops 50 IQ points—not a good situation.

Since there is no specific diagnosis for the inflexible child, many mental health professionals and pediatricians tend to diagnose these children with any of the following: attention deficit hyperactivity disorder (ADHD), Asperger's syndrome, pervasive developmental disorder, depression, oppositional-defiant disorder, or anxiety.

The techniques we outline in this book will help you deal with an inflexible child, though it will probably take longer to make progress than with other children because inflexible kids need more help (and time) in developing new skills.

We find that inflexible children usually respond to the technique of Academies (see Chapter 20). This appears to cement the desired behavior in their minds.

Also, we often find the best way to help an inflexible child is to focus on just a few bad behaviors and break the desired results into smaller chunks. This makes the change more gradual and easier for him to accept. However, the basic attitude you adopt toward an inflexible child is the same as with any other defiant kid: You need to be consistent and follow a plan if you want to change his behavior. Getting mad at the child doesn't work and splashes fuel on the fire.

Chapter

3

Because I Said So

How Your Parenting Style
Can Lead to Defiance

Shocked to see the subtitle of this chapter? Thought it was all your
kid's fault for being difficult?

Surprise!

We have found that parents can trigger defiant behavior in several ways:

▶ by trying to exercise significant control over a child
▶ by trying too hard to maintain peace or harmony
▶ by being so apprehensive of the potential legal consequences
of disciplining a child that they are afraid to set appropriate
limits.

It's easy for any parent to get caught in these types of mistakes
occasionally—we've made them too—but if you consistently react in
one of these ways, you'll end up encouraging your child's defiance

17

rather than ending it. Let's look at some specific examples of how this plays out.

The "Defiant" Parent

Defiant parents tend to expect perfect compliance from their children, and they often micromanage their children. They not only tell their children what to do, they also insist on telling them precisely *how* to do it. They expect their wisdom to rub off on their children so the kids won't make the same mistakes or suffer hardships similar to the ones they did as kids. When their children challenge an order, these parents respond with "I told you so; that's why."

An example of this control process took place with a family that Ray counseled recently. A mother of four grew very angry with her oldest, who she believed was being defiant. Ray didn't agree. To him, it looked like the mom's personality was so difficult that she was forcing her son to revolt.

The situation came to a head this way: The child was asked to vacuum his room. He took a handheld minivac to do the job. As he walked toward his room, his mother reamed him out because she wanted it done with the upright vacuum.

Her complaint centered around the way she wanted it done: She felt that the vacuum her son chose was too small for the job and would double the amount of time that it would take to clean the room. But the truly important issue should have been whether or not the room got cleaned, not how long it took. So Ray asked the mother, "If you want the room cleaned, what difference does it make whether he cleans it with an upright or a minivac or just sucks the dirt up with a straw?"

In normal development, children need to master their own bodies and environments at their own paces. They need to be the ones choosing which methods they'll use to do their own chores and tasks. Most of all, children need to learn from their own mistakes—not the mistakes of their elders.

When you tell people what to do and follow it up with how to do it, the basic human reaction is to revolt and say "Try and make me!" or "You're not my boss!" Insisting on having something done a certain way rather than looking at the end result can create a defiant, oppositional response in your child.

The Peacemaker Parent

Peacemaking parents can't handle much negativity. They are the meek, the peacemakers. They may inherit the Earth, but before they do, their difficult kids will drive them round the bend. Seriously, anger can be very stressful for these parents. It may simply make them uncomfortable for any of a variety of reasons, or remind them of their own troubled childhood.

These parents may think that if the household is not harmonious, it reflects negatively on them. So they will do almost anything to appease their children and keep the peace.

A client of Ray's had this problem: She wanted absolutely no fighting in her household. Whenever her son would get upset—yelling and screaming at her—she'd give in and buy him whatever he wanted, from a new computer game to $140 Nike Airs.

Then there was the problem that Bill had with Teddy, a "defiant" dog he used to own. Just like defiant children, Teddy knew exactly how to motivate Bill to do what he wanted him to do. He had been an "inside" dog when Bill got him from the previous owner, but Teddy had a problem with urinating on the walls of the house, so Bill decided to put him outside.

As soon as he was left alone outside, Teddy began to whine in an annoying tone. Bill knew that it would get better if he just waited the dog out. Rather than quieting down, Teddy began to whine at a higher pitch. Bill began to worry that the dog would upset the neighbors. Finally, Teddy reached a fever pitch that Bill could stand no longer. So Bill let him in.

Teddy quickly learned that when he worked his way to that one unbearable noise, Bill would crumble and let him inside. It took him 45 minutes to get to that pitch the first time, but he soon got to where he'd reach that annoying tone the second that Bill closed the door. Eventually, Bill would let the dog out, hear the whine, and open the door right back up so Teddy could come back in. Teddy had put the choke collar on *Bill.* He knew exactly how to get what he wanted from Bill. He made Bill more motivated to change than he was.

This is exactly what your defiant child can do to you.

Like Teddy, a defiant child is a master at making scenes in public. He knows that if he cries just a little louder at the grocery store, you'll cave in and buy him a Milky Way because you're worried about what other people think. He may care about what other people think too, but not nearly as much as you.

Defiant kids are willing to escalate the process to such a ferocious pitch that you can't stand it anymore. And it doesn't end just because they reach their teenage years. One mother who brought her 13-year-old son in for counseling told us about a scene the son made one time when he went golfing. When she refused to rent him a golf cart to ride around in, he pitched a screaming fit in front of all his teenage friends. The mother and the teenage friends were embarrassed, but the son was not. He was focused on getting what he wanted, just like Teddy.

When you respond as a peacemaker to tantrums like this, you're just as likely to help mold a defiant child as parents who play the defiant parent role.

The Apprehensive Parent

Apprehensive parents are afraid to discipline for fear that others will see what they're doing as child abuse. Now, we're not talking about beating a child or physically harming him, just using appropriate techniques such as Time Out restraint to help the child learn. Some parents are afraid to take even basic steps like that.

We remember one mother who used to exemplify the "apprehensive parent" attitude. She had used appropriate physical discipline on her kids when they were little, but she grew afraid of correcting her younger son after an incident at her older son's Little League baseball game.

The younger son grew restless watching his brother from the stands. Although he had toys to occupy his time, he quickly found more innovative ways to occupy himself, including wandering off and throwing pebbles at passing cars. The mother warned him several times to behave and sit beside her, but she soon was forced to put him in Time

Out next to the stands. Upset with his mother, the young boy began cursing loudly at her, and he tried to leave Time Out.

His mother assertively restrained him from leaving the Time Out area, which only led to louder and more difficult yelling from the lad. Right about then, two women in the stands looked around to see what all the commotion was about. Concerned, one of the women warned this mother that she would report her to Child Protective Services if she didn't release her son.

The mother, overwhelmed and feeling as if she was being attacked on two fronts, released her child. Her son then felt even more powerful and responded to his newly acquired power by acting even more obnoxious. And his mother became very apprehensive about correcting her son in public again.

There are many things that can trigger an apprehensive attitude. It can be the result of encounters with well-intentioned strangers—like the women in the bleachers—who believe that they are standing up for the "rights" of children. Also, in our practices, we frequently hear com-

BEHAVIOR BASICS

Three Parenting Styles Likely to Produce or Aggravate Defiance

1. *Defiant parents.* These people micromanage and come down too hard on kids. Making every issue a control issue is bound to create more opposition and defiance.
2. *Peacemaker parents.* For varying reasons, these parents will cough up money or stretch themselves to their outer limits— all to avoid conflict.
3. *Apprehensive parents.* Overly concerned about interference from other parents or outside agencies such as Child Protective Services, these parents don't provide their kids with appropriate discipline and end up parenting out of fear.

plaints that defiant children themselves have used the threat of a call to Child Protective Services in attempts to avoid their parents' discipline. Finally, parents may become afraid to discipline because they've read in some parenting book that good parents are not supposed to use anything other than reason or rewards to deal with children—otherwise, they might traumatize their children.

If you have doubts about your ability to discipline appropriately, seek a counselor's advice. But don't give up appropriate discipline as a tool to teach your child to behave. That, ultimately, is bad for the child.

When we parents are afraid of disciplining, or when we parent out of fear, we allow our children to have the upper hand and don't show our children the proper guidance that comes naturally when we parent from a basis of love.

Other Influences

Three Things That Can Trigger
Your Child's Rebellion

Sometimes, it's not so much what's inside your child that makes him defiant as it is the situations around him. Hectic life schedules, crises and transitions, and the way you may respond to your child's misbehavior all can create situations that lock the two of you into power struggles. By understanding and planning ahead, you can avoid many of these skirmishes.

The first trigger for most of us is simply the modern era in which we live. Most of us have no time! Society demands more hours from us than it did from our parents and grandparents. In order to "get ahead," many of us feel compelled to arrive early for work and stay late. Then there's soccer practice, religious activities, and dozens more attractions all vying for our time.

As a result, we parents look more and more to a schedule to keep our lives organized. We need to get up at such-and-such a time, we plan to eat breakfast within a brief window of time, and we expect our kids to be bathed, dressed, and ready to go on our schedule.

The problem is, strategies like this don't work in a child's world. You have already mastered your motor skills. You know how long it takes to fix your hair or knot your tie. But your kid hasn't achieved mastery yet. Kids have their own time frame, and expecting them to meet yours can lead to trouble.

Jessica, for example, was constantly butting heads with her mother, Martha, because the youngster was making her mother late for work. But when Martha was asked to describe a time when things went better in the morning, the cause of the problem—and the solution to it—were clear.

"Oh, there were a few mornings when I used my flextime at work to get an extra 15 minutes," she began, a light flickering on in her mind. "That extra 15 minutes gave my daughter all the time she needed to get ready. You know, we hardly had any problems when I did that. Wonder why I haven't done that more often."

Understanding that your child isn't always on your time schedule—and allowing you both more time to get ready each morning—is essential to avoiding unnecessary power struggles.

Crisis and Transition

On the road of life, we all ride over some bumpy asphalt now and then. Some bumps are more predictable than others. The death of a parent, the death of a grandparent, or moving to a new school are situations that can cause crises in kids' lives, and each crisis leads to stress. But problems in life don't need to reach crisis level to be stressful: Even going through puberty or moving to a bigger house can trigger a stress reaction.

When stress hits, some kids will become defiant in response. You can tell that their reactions are related to a situation because their change in attitude takes place over a brief period of time—anywhere from a couple of days to a couple of months—and close to the time of the stress.

For example, Joey was a normal, run-of-the-mill kid in first and second grades—and he rarely caused problems. But when his parents had marital conflict and divorced during his fourth-grade year, he became uncharacteristically defiant in a short period of time. Joey clearly was responding to a situation.

If you notice this kind of behavior change, we recommend that you follow the guidelines in this book *and* take your child in for counseling as soon as possible.

How the Cycle of Power Struggles Feeds Itself

Kids from age 2 through age 4 are defiant. Take it to the bank. That's where we get the term *Terrible Twos*. It's a normal stage during which most kids try to exert their influence and control. Very often, they challenge their parents. By the time they reach age 5, children have usually passed through this stage and are ready to listen to their parents—at least a good portion of the time. But that improvement depends largely on how the parents handle defiance during the Terrible Twos stage and the years that follow.

If you don't properly manage misbehavior when your child is young, he will learn how to get away with not doing what you are asking him to do.

When that happens, you and your child wind up in a power struggle: Your child will try to coax you into not following through with a command, and you will try to coax your child to comply.

Imagine you and your child playing tug-of-war with a knot tied in the middle of the rope. You are each saying to the other, "You drop the rope first, and we can untie the knot." But neither of you is willing to let go first. So you end up in a stalemate.

Who loses in that situation? You do, because you don't get him to do what you want him to do.

A child often learns to avoid complying by seeing how his parents handle interactions. And as "The Cycle of Defiance" on page 26 shows, acts of defiance feed on themselves.

After parents state a command, the child either complies or doesn't. If the child does comply, then the parents do other things besides struggle with him. See the arrow pointing to the right at the top

The Cycle of Defiance

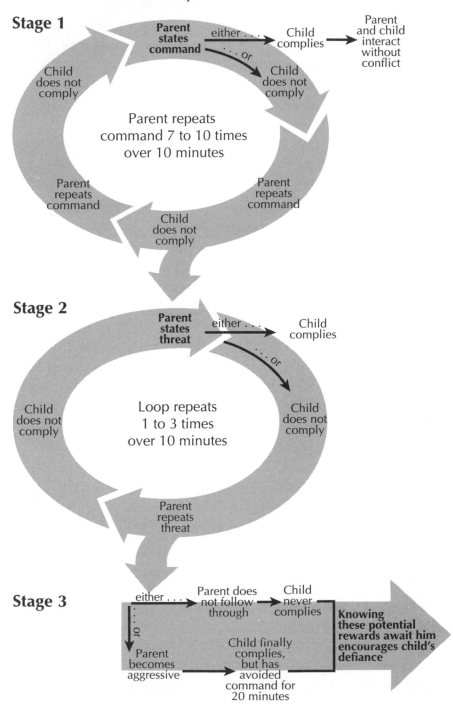

Stage 1

Parent states command — either... → Child complies → Parent and child interact without conflict

...or → Child does not comply

Parent repeats command 7 to 10 times over 10 minutes

Child does not comply

Parent repeats command

Parent repeats command

Child does not comply

Stage 2

Parent states threat — either... → Child complies

...or → Child does not comply

Loop repeats 1 to 3 times over 10 minutes

Child does not comply

Parent repeats threat

Stage 3

either... → Parent does not follow through → Child never complies

...or → Parent becomes aggressive → Child finally complies, but has avoided command for 20 minutes

Knowing these potential rewards await him encourages child's defiance

of the table? No problem. But if the youngster disobeys, most parents tend to repeat the command. Somehow, we come to the conclusion that our children have basketball-size balls of wax in their ears.

Many children get hearing tests because parents believe that there is really something wrong with their auditory canals. In reality, all that's happening is selective listening. Kids are picking out what they want to hear. Are you with us so far?

"The Cycle of Defiance" says that most parents repeat commands 7 to 10 times, but we parents have been known to repeat ourselves as many as 10 to 15 times. We may not repeat the exact words that many times, but we bring the matter to our kids' attention on at least that many separate occasions. For example, if you stand in front of the television, clear your throat, or just state your child's name, you may as well be repeating your command because your child knows what you're implying.

Every time you repeat a command, your voice likely gets louder. In response, your child's voice also gets louder. If you say, "Junior, I'm not going to tell you anymore: Turn that video game off and do your homework!," his response will escalate from ignoring you to replying, "I said in a minute. Quit bugging me!"

So the emotional volume in the household increases dramatically. All the while, *the stopwatch is running.*

This sequence of repeating commands takes, on average, 10 minutes. Rather than producing the desired result, it helps your child learn that if he delays and yells, or if he simply doesn't do what has been asked of him, he gets to do what he wants for 10 more minutes. Nice payoff, huh?

When we parents tire of giving unheeded commands, we typically move on to threats. And once we start slinging threats, we're treading into dangerous territory.

First, there is the risk of ruining our own credibility if we make empty threats, like threatening to throw away the television if your child doesn't start his homework. Or consider what one of Bill's clients told her child: She threatened to make him sleep in a graveyard if he didn't go to bed. As she delivered that threat, the boy just rolled his eyes. He knew how serious his mother was about following through on that bluff.

Take another look at "The Cycle of Defiance" and you'll see that when things reach the threat stage, parents normally repeat a threat only one to three times and wait longer between repetitions than they do with commands. The big problem is that it takes another good chunk of time to state a threat and then follow through. On average, that adds another 10 minutes to the tug-of-war. What does this teach a child? If he waits and refuses to comply for a while, he can now get something like 20 more minutes off before he has to comply or deal with you about the matter.

If a child does eventually comply, most adults usually hold a grudge. And if the child does not comply, then parents tend to commit one of two mistakes: Either they get too physically or verbally aggressive with the child, or they fail to follow through on the threat.

BEHAVIOR BASICS

Circumstances Likely to Produce Defiant Children

1. *Time-crunched parents.* We expect children to comply instantly because, with our busy, chaotic lifestyles, we have no time to spare or argue. Kids don't always have the capability or interest in changing as quickly as our lives demand.
2. *Crises or transitions in the child's or family's life.* Sometimes, defiance is a temporary or emotional response by the child to situational changes such as moving to a new school or a new town, going through puberty, or parents going through a divorce.
3. *Parents responding inappropriately to defiance.* When parents get hooked into an ineffective response to defiance, they inadvertently set up the conditions for more misbehavior. Children learn that they can escape from compliance by using various delay maneuvers and by getting the parents frustrated or upset.

Two-thirds of the time, parents do the latter, and strong-willed children—who are usually good gamblers—will take those odds. (Think about it; these odds are quite a bit better than the state lotteries that many of us play.) Kids have learned that they can refuse to do anything an adult wants as long as they can tolerate the negative energy that comes with not complying.

Nothing about the defiant behavior illustrated in "The Cycle of Defiance" is biochemical or genetic. This is entirely a learned response. This is a pattern of behavior that your child probably has learned by observing the tone of your voice, the color of your face, and the amount of time that has passed since you first made the threat. From these observations, your child can distinguish how serious you are and whether you are bluffing. What has he learned? He's learned that if he can tolerate the negativity, then he can get or do what he wants most of the time.

Chapter

Why Aren't These Kids Motivated to Change?

The Differences between Garlic and Beans, Horses and Camels

A simple way to understand why your defiant child doesn't seem motivated to do what you ask is to realize that there are two kinds of problems: Garlic Problems and Bean Problems. When you eat garlic, the smell won't bother you because you can't detect your own breath. But the people around you can know that you're coming from a mile away. On the other hand, let's say that you eat some beans—an entire bowlful. That creates a problem that both you and those around you will notice.

Defiant kids have a Garlic Problem. They may see havoc swirling around them, but they're convinced that somebody else started it. In fact, when put on the spot, they'll quickly and wholeheartedly respond, "I don't have a problem."

This is a major difference between defiant and depressed children.

Both can be very stubborn, argumentative, and negative, and it seems that both want to control everything. But depressed children will usually not delight in conflict. They will tell you, in some way, that they are bothered or upset by a situation. So, depressed children may suffer from a Bean Problem—a condition where both they and others are aware of the problem—but not a Garlic Problem.

It's like a popular story that we heard about a well-known tycoon/politician. He was driving his cigarette boat (a long, sleek, fast vehicle) across Lake Texoma, which is near Dallas. He took it straight out of the dock and headed for point B, his destination. In the process of getting there, he drove directly in front of another boat's bow even though the other boat had the right of way. He just went right in front of the other boat, couldn't care less, because all he cared about was his destination. If someone else got in his way, tough!—or, as adolescents like to say, "Talk to the hand!" There was no consideration like, "Gee, if I don't look out for others, somebody could get hurt." Other people's destinations were not important to him.

Whether they are tycoons or children, strong-willed people are not as into what other people think of them as they are into getting their needs met.

When we ask in the first therapy session, "What do you want to get out of these sessions, what are you here for, and what do you want to change?," the defiant child often responds, "Nothing." A baffled expression normally accompanies this reply, similar to how you might stare at a mechanic who wants to overhaul the engine on your brand-new car. Your response would probably be, "Why would I want to fix my car when there is nothing wrong with it?"

That look remains on the child's face as he answers questions such as:

"How about school . . . things going okay?"

"Oh yeah."

"How about home . . . things going okay?"

"They're going fine."

It's never a problem for the young troublemaker. But the parents, who have been sitting in on the session, bear looks of amazement throughout this dialogue. So we ask the parents, "Well, what is going on?"

Often, they rage about recent incidents that have escalated into severe conflicts in the parents' eyes. And the kid will reply, "Well, yeah, but . . . ," always wearing an expression on his face like "that's not really my problem." These kids say things like: "The teacher has the problem." "You have the problem." "That was just one time." "It was no big deal."

All of these are classic symptoms of a Garlic Problem.

Want a real-life example? Take the case of Jason, who has been in counseling on and off for 4 years. Every year, without fail, about the middle of the school year, he has a major blowup with one of his instructors. This year, it was a problem with Mrs. Thomas, and the dis-cussion between Ray and Jason went like this:

"Jason, what's going on?"

"Well, Mrs. Thomas lies and cheats. Everyone knows she lies. She's an awful teacher. She's the worst teacher I ever had."

"Jason, every year you say the same thing about whatever teacher you have that year. Last year, it was Mrs. Jones."

"Yeah. She was pretty bad."

"And how about Mr. Admont the year before? And then there were Mrs. Taylor and Mrs. Adkins. Remember how bad you said they were?"

"Sure. Seems like they pick out a worse one for me each year."

"Wow! In 5 years of school, you have had the worst teachers avail-able in each grade. That must be some kind of a record!"

"Yeah, it's a bitch, isn't it?"

Throughout this conversation, Jason showed no awareness that he might be adding something negative to the situation. His attitude was, "I'm okay, but everyone else needs to get their act together." He saw himself as the victim of a lousy school system and even worse teachers.

This is a classic case of a Garlic Problem. In order to end a Garlic Problem, you must give kids like this a problem that mainly bothers them—not you. In part 3, we will outline ways to transfer the problem to your child and make him an expert problem solver.

Horses and Camels: Positive vs. Negative Motivation

A simple way to understand what motivates a defiant child is to compare two animals: horses and camels.

Horses tend to be *positively motivated* animals. They like to please their masters, and they're willing to work in exchange for some praise or a sugar cube or some other form of food. You could attach a stick to a horse's head and dangle a carrot 2 feet in front of its eyes. The horse would move ceaselessly toward the food without realizing that it was getting no closer.

Horses are good work animals, but they cannot survive in certain environments. Let's say that you need to cross the Sahara Desert and you take a horse with you. In the extreme temperatures of a desert, horses won't work for long. They most likely will dehydrate and die in a hurry. "Bummer!," as defiant children say.

That's why most Arabs use camels to get work accomplished in the desert. These animals aren't as pretty or as easy to ride as horses, but their ability to get by in extreme heat is remarkable.

Unlike the horse, a camel is *negatively motivated*. In the middle of a desert crossing, a camel might decide to plop down on the sand and take a beauty rest. You could get down on your knees and offer a variety of enticements, but to no avail. Reasoning with this camel about water up ahead wouldn't cause him to rise.

Pretend that the camel could speak, and here's what he'd say: "Hey, I don't need any water. I've got all the water I need. See that big hump on my back? Thanks for sharing, though."

Food would be an equally ineffective motivator.

"I've got plenty of that in my hump too," the camel would say. "Don't worry a bit about me. You go right on down the trail; I'll be fine."

If the camel could understand English, you could try scaring him by talking about the vicious sand storms that arise in deserts. The howling wind carries razor-sharp sand at blistering speeds with enough force to rip human skin apart.

"Aw, I've got some mighty tough hide," the camel would reply, also blinking each of its many layers of eyelids that protect its pupils from the blowing grains of sand.

Then you could try yanking on its harness. His response? "Yeah, feel free to try and drag 800 pounds of me through this sand."

No, camels can't be bought off with bribes. They need a different style of encouragement.

A trained rider knows this, so when the camel he's riding decides to take a siesta in the Sahara, he doesn't get upset. He simply pulls out some sticks of wood and a shovel from the camel's purse and proceeds toward the camel's tail. Under the camel's butt, he digs a hole, drops in the sticks, and strikes a match. Pretty soon, the camel feels something unpleasant (fire penetrating the tough hide on its buttocks) and rather quickly decides to do something to get away from that pain.

Many defiant children more closely resemble camels than horses. When a parent or teacher tries to approach them the way riders approach horses—by reasoning with them or enticing them or explaining to them precisely why they need to complete a specific task—these kids let you know quickly that they're not going to react like horses.

In fact, these kids often prefer negative reactions. Their need for control is extensive, and watching a parent or teacher do flips or set up behavior charts may be more satisfying to them than actually completing the tasks that they've been asked to do.

Also, as we discussed in "Where Defiance Starts" on pages 13–14, a defiant child's ability to tolerate negativity is much higher than that of any parent or teacher. He can take all the condescending comments you may toss his way.

Blending Positive and Negative Motivations

When you want your child to stop acting like a camel, you need to find some way to light a fire under him. (Not literally. Tempting as it might sound, don't go take a blowtorch to your son's behind.) To figuratively light that fire, you must provide a good mix of negative consequences to help complement the positive enticements you usually use to motivate him.

This system of positives and negatives succeeds because it appeals to the two things that inspire all of us to act differently: the desire to avoid pain and the desire to experience pleasure.

Generally, we humans change for only two reasons: Either we want something badly enough, or we want to get away from a situation badly enough. (See "What Makes Us Do the Things We Do?" on page 11.)

If we want money, status, sex, education, or anything else, we will do whatever it takes to acquire it. But if we come upon certain unpleasant situations, we can be inspired to change simply because we don't like the unpleasantness. If we're driving along a highway, for example, and smell the stench of a paper mill or sewage station, we are tempted to push the gas pedal and speed past the odor. Likewise, we might be negatively motivated by hunger, pain, boredom, harm, or danger.

When it comes to defiant children, we've seen a mix of positive and negative motivations help dozens of them. Take young Josh. His mother, Paula, was raised in a family that got along well except for an occasional quarrel between her older sister and herself. Her brother was usually overprotective and rarely argued with her. Soon after Josh was born, Paula realized that she was going into strange and unfamiliar territory. Josh "had a mind of his own" early on. As an infant, he launched into tantrums that lasted for more than an hour. By the time he reached the ripe old age of 10, he had the entire household revolving around his needs.

Paula tried a number of strategies for dealing with him and his temper. She tried talking him through his tantrums and she attempted to avoid conflicts. She also tried to alter his behavior by using many different forms of behavior charts that rewarded him for positive changes. By the time she first visited Bill, she had exhausted all of her resources and all of the wonderful suggestions that her extended family had to offer.

Bill explained that approaching Josh with positive reinforcement alone wasn't getting his attention or holding him accountable—something Josh desperately needed.

What Paula needed to do, said Bill, was make Josh responsible for

Preparing Your Child for the Real World

Blending positive and negative motivation doesn't just improve a child's behavior. It plays an important part in shaping the child for life as an adult.

In the "real world," he'll face positive and negative motivation all the time. For example, many of us work because we enjoy the pay and derive some internal satisfaction from our jobs (positive motivation). And then there is negative motivation, which stimulates people to work in order to avoid being homeless and hungry and living under a bridge.

Another example: Let's say that you wanted to buy a new home. Likely, this will be the largest single investment that you will make in your life. And if you want a really nice home, you wind up with a pretty hefty payment each month—a payment that very well may stretch you to your financial limits every now and then.

It's not so hard to write that check the first few months while the house is new and you're setting the house up just how you want it. That is like positive motivation. But 3 or 4 years down the road—when the toilet's leaking, the paint's chipping, the roof needs some new shingles—you may not be so excited about mailing that monthly payment. That's where the bank puts negative motivation into play. Either you send that payment or a loan officer comes out to foreclose on the house.

Many events in real life have positive and negative motivations attached to them. If you attempt to raise your child using only positive motivators, you are not preparing him for the world that exists outside your home. This is an important point that you'll notice us emphasizing throughout this book. Children must be adequately prepared to live in the real world. (Unless, of course, you plan to care for them for the rest of their lives.)

his behavior and impose consequences when Josh misbehaved. Paula tried this new philosophy and soon saw a noticeable and steady improvement in Josh.

Paula admitted that initially she was afraid to put negative consequences on Josh's behavior for fear of squashing his spirit and hurting his self-esteem. She now understands that by simply trying to bribe Josh into good behavior, she was allowing him to misbehave and walk all over her while, at the same time, leaving him feeling out of control and awful about himself. Josh needed the negative consequences of his behaviors just as much as he required the positive ones.

Defiant kids are not usually motivated to change simply because someone else wants them to. This is something that many therapists, parents, and teachers don't realize. They hold "carrots" in front of children in attempts to get them to talk and move toward enlightenment, awareness, and better behavior. But this approach doesn't work, because defiant children already know how to get what they want, and it has nothing to do with positive motivation.

These kids are quite comfortable and have no particular desire to change what they're doing. They don't believe that they have a problem. And conflict, as uncomfortable as it may seem to others, either doesn't bother them as much as it does other people, or else bothers them so little that they get over it more quickly than do the adults who are doing the yelling and punishing.

As you consider this concept, keep in mind that while defiant kids are more like camels, they will not respond *only* to negatives. They need a blend of positives and negatives. If you taunt your child with positives (or negatives) alone, you will end up frustrated and your child will remain unchanged. Understanding this concept is vital to changing your situation.

A popular comic book character from the days when we were growing up—Alfred E. Neuman—used as his motto the question "What, me worry?" In a similar fashion, a defiant child who discovers that his parents are more motivated than he is to have him do well in

BEHAVIOR BASICS

Camels with Garlic Problems

Defiant children often don't recognize that they have a problem. They tend to think that others around them are the source of difficulties. In this way, they have Garlic Problems that bother others—not necessarily themselves.

Most children are aware of the problems they are causing other people and feel bad about causing those problems. Those are more like Bean Problems.

Defiant, strong-willed children also identify more with camels, which at times need external motivation to cooperate, than they do with horses, who are more naturally and easily cooperative. Camels respond to a combination of positive and negative incentives, not to merely mild disapproval.

school or succeed in a host of other things may silently make a similar comment: "What, me motivated?"

Most children, like many adults, prefer the path of least resistance. If someone else is going to be more worried about the problem and more motivated to solve it, children will gladly step aside and let that person handle things.

Part 2

Who Has Control of This Joystick?

All of us adults have ideas on how to parent. Though we hate to admit it, most of us parent either similarly to how we were raised or exactly the opposite. Neither is usually the best strategy in this ever-changing world. Yet we hold on to our parenting ideas with such tenacity that we often fail to see how these ideas contribute to the problems that we experience with our children.

This is especially an issue for people who are trying to parent a defiant child. If you allow dysfunctional "dances" and inappropriate "myths" to rule you when you're parenting a defiant child, you'll find it much harder to help your child.

The point is *not* that your parenting ideas are completely wrong, or that you're inadequate if you use some of these methods. We've used them too. But we've learned that they don't work—that they get in the way of good parenting. In this section we'll explain why dances and myths fail with defiant kids like yours. Then, we can get into methods that really do work.

May I Have This Dance?

The Eight Ways Your Child Struts
a Mambo around Your Rules

When we talk about dances in the title of this chapter, we're not referring to the rhythmic shuffling of feet and clasping of arms that love-stricken couples might engage in at a country-western club. No, as Ron Taffel, Ph.D., suggests in his book *Parenting by Heart*, these dances are patterns of behavior that parents often adopt while trying to get kids to change, and they're definitely dances you want to avoid.

Why? Because when you dance with your child, your actions become highly predictable, allowing your child to pinpoint exactly how to manipulate you. Not every parent and child have the same dance, but most will use one of these eight popular variations.

The Guilt Dance. This dance has changed a lot since your childhood years. When you were growing up, adults took the lead in this dance. Parents used to make the child feel guilty about not doing homework or failing to do some household chore. They'd say something like, "In my days, we didn't have the opportunity to go to school. We had to first work in the field, and if there was any time left over, then we were delighted to attend school. You don't appreciate how easy it is now!" After enough of that, you'd often do whatever your parents wanted.

These days, it's often the child who takes the lead in the Guilt Dance.

Numerous times in therapy, parents will tell us about guilt trips that their children have put on them. A kid may say, "You've been at work all day. I was lonely and bored. I want to rent a video game now." So the parent rents the video game. Then there's our favorite Guilt Dance, the one where a child says, "I can't do math, remember? I have ADHD [attention deficit hyperactivity disorder]!"

In both cases, the child is using guilt to make the parents do what he wants. With defiant kids, the last thing you want to do is let them control you with guilt because they are experts at manipulating this dance.

The Whining Dance. In this one, the child will work you with his vocal cords. He gets his voice keyed up to where it sounds like nails scratching a blackboard. For example: "But you said I could sit in the front seat, Moommeeeee!" is a popular whine. Or a child may wail, "But you promised me a cookie!" Adults often give in just to get some peace. Remember Bill's dog Teddy? None of us are safe from this one.

If you ever want the whining in your house to stop, you must avoid this dance.

The Bargaining Dance. This is the dance where your 7-year-old uses the negotiating strategies of a United Nations Peacekeeping Committee to get his way. Example: You've been on Junior for half an hour to stop the games and start his homework. His response: "Just one more level of Nintendo, and *then* I'll start my homework." Unfortunately, most of us have been guilty of caving in to this dance.

The dangers of allowing your child to bargain for what he wants can range from an annoyance in the early years to much more serious problems when he becomes a teenager.

The Abusive Dance. This one is very common among defiant youngsters. They will become either verbally or physically abusive toward their parents in order to provoke an angry response, so the parents will then feel guilty.

Defiant kids often use this dance to seek revenge for being corrected or having limits set on them. For example, when 14-year-old Sara was mad at her mother, she would call her a foul name—especially in public. Once home, the mother would rage and sometimes slap Sara. Mom would then feel guilty and give in to one of Sara's demands. As a child ages, the Abusive Dance gets more serious, nastier, and sometimes more lethal.

The Unenforceable Dance. This is a very problematic dance, and all kinds of families fall victim to its beat. It is common in families where there has been a divorce. One example is the divorced father who only saw his kids once a month. After one visit, he found out that his 16-year-old son had wrecked a car, so he told the teenager, "You're grounded!" There was no way that the father could enforce this since he didn't live with his son, so the boy shrugged it off.

With the Unenforceable Dance, children lose respect for their parents because they know that their parents' word is mud.

The Perry Mason Dance. This is our favorite. It happens when parents try to get their children to show guilt and remorse for some behavior by using the old Perry Mason interrogation technique. You remember that one—Perry used to get his witness to admit guilt on the stand in the final moments of a show. It often would go something like this:

SITUATION: *Mr. Smith was dead at the beginning of the show. Perry knows that Miss Jones did it, but she won't admit to it. Perry begins questioning Miss Jones.*

PERRY MASON: *So, Miss Jones, you say that you didn't know the deceased Mr. Smith?*

MISS JONES: *I knew that he was the chairman of our company, but I didn't see him anywhere except maybe in the break room.*

PERRY MASON: *So, Miss Jones, you're saying that other than him being your boss, you had no relationship with the deceased at all?*

MISS JONES (SMILING NERVOUSLY): *No, not at all. Nothing except maybe pouring him coffee in the break room.*

PERRY MASON (GOES TO THE TABLE, PULLS OUT A SHEET OF PAPER, AND HANDS IT TO MISS JONES): *Then, Miss Jones, can you tell me what these are?*

MISS JONES (LOOKS AT THE RESTAURANT RECEIPT, REALIZES THAT IT IS DATED THE NIGHT OF THE MURDER, AND SEES AN ATTACHED PHOTO THAT SHOWS BOTH HER AND THE VICTIM LEAVING THAT RESTAURANT; HER FACE TURNS SOUR): *You're right. I admit it. We were having an affair. We had dinner together, and he wouldn't leave his wife, so I shot him. I killed him! I wish the whole thing had never happened!*

So often, parents try to play Perry Mason and extract similar confessions of guilt, remorse, and accountability from kids. Unfortunately, home is not a courtroom. When kids feel that they are being grilled, they do not become more open and admit their shortcomings. Instead, they become more defensive and noncompliant.

The Therapist Dance. This is the one where the parent adopts an empathetic tone and tries to act like a psychologist. (Our own children often fall victim to this dance.) For example, a parent Ray counseled noticed that her child was tearing up the living room one day. In response, the mother walked up to him, struck a "Thinker" statue pose, and wondered softly aloud: "I wonder what Mikey's feeling so angry about right now." She was amazed that his behavior continued.

Trying to arouse insight does not create behavior change in a defiant child, and it often leads to more frustration.

The Terrorist Dance. This is the one where a child plays terrorist and threatens to harm himself. For example, Billy, who was 11, didn't like the way that his parents were starting to set limits on him. One day, his mother picked him up from school and started asking about his day. Billy casually mentioned that his day went well, and that in gym class, Coach Akin had talked about a child who attempted suicide because his parents were being too firm with him.

Naturally, the mother freaked out. She told Ray how afraid she was that her son would kill himself if she set any more limits. Ray calmed her down and told her that Billy was in no danger. The boy was using this ploy to get her to back off. Once his mother understood this, Billy's manipulative attempts became benign.

BEHAVIOR BASICS

Popular Steps in the Dance of Defiance

Guilt Dance. The child uses the parent's guilt to get what he wants.

Whining Dance. The child wears his parents down by whining until they relent.

Bargaining Dance. The child bargains with the finesse of a professional mediator for what he wants or to avoid consequences.

Abusive Dance. The child gets physically or verbally violent to see if he can control his environment and intimidate people into letting him do what he wants.

Unenforceable Dance. The parent threatens burdensome consequences that are impossible to carry out.

Perry Mason Dance. The parent uses reason and words in an attempt to coerce a confession and have the child take responsibility for his actions.

Therapist Dance. The parent tries to listen sympathetically when the child misbehaves or tries to get the child to discover his underlying feelings that led to the misbehavior, thinking that insight alone will curb misbehavior.

Terrorist Dance. The child makes subtle or obvious threats of running away, committing suicide or violence, or some other scary possibility to try to get the parent to relent.

When parents respond to threats, they are parenting out of fear and not parenting out of love. This becomes unsettling for the child also.

The danger with all these dances is that after a few run-throughs, your child can predict what you will say or do in each case. Kids know that information is power. When your child can predict how you as the parent will respond, that gives him control over a situation.

Later, we'll show you how to cut in on those dances and form some more appropriate ones—ones where you take the lead.

Parenting Mythology

How Your Beliefs Can Undermine the Way You Raise Your Child

Sometimes, the way we analyze a problem keeps us entrenched in it.

Let's say that you aren't getting along with your mother-in-law. If you fall into the myth that "she just won't change," she probably never will. In fact, the divide between the two of you is likely to spread to the size of the Grand Canyon before things get better.

But if you set aside your beliefs, start thinking of her as a reasonable person, and brainstorm ways to get along, you'll be amazed at how quickly she'll become one of your avid supporters.

It's just a matter of stamping out the myth and acting on the reality.

The same holds true for parenting a defiant child. If you accept myths about what defiant kids can and cannot do, it will stall your attempts to help your child learn to behave. It's only when you put those myths aside that you begin to make progress.

Here are a few of the worst myths that we've seen in our years of counseling—and the realities.

Myth: Nothing Works with These Kids

Does it seem as if you are up against insurmountable odds and that your child is unchangeable—just plain bad? If so, you have been caught up in one of the many parent myths, the "can't" myth.

You know how this one goes. It's just one endless battle after another: Your son consistently ignores your calls that bedtime has arrived, or your daughter always gives you a blank stare after being told to stop pulling out her brother's hair. If you deal with enough of this, you may begin to think that your child is just wired to do the wrong thing and that there is nothing you can do about it.

You may even reach a point where you throw your hands into the air and exclaim: "Nothing works with these kids!" And if you give in to that way of thinking, you may decide to accept and cope with your child the way he is, figuring that he has a genetic deficit or is suffering from "broken chromosomes"—something that happened when he was conceived. That's a dangerous direction to take.

Sometimes, parents who fall victim to this myth tell us that their children have attention deficit hyperactivity disorder (ADHD), which prevents the youngsters from understanding how their actions lead to consequences. Balderdash! Of course it's possible for ADHD kids to understand consequences and learn from them. Often, they need the help of medication and therapy, but they can learn.

The truth is, all kids *can* change. They are not incorrigible. They just need appropriate training to break their bad habits. When you accept the myth that "nothing works," it disables you from discovering an antidote to your child's behavior.

Myth: What These Kids Need Is a Good Whop

Do you remember your first spanking? Not the first time you gave your child one, but the first time your parents brightened your buttocks with a wooden paddle or leather belt. It may have worked like the "hot stove" theory: You were told not to touch the red coil atop the oven, you did it anyway, your hand burned like the dickens, and you never touched a stove—hot or cold—the rest of your childhood years. Or maybe you were told not to throw a baseball in the house and you promptly missed your brother's mitt, squarely hit Mom's crystal hummingbird figurine, got your hide tanned, and waited 10 weeks before touching that white Spalding indoors or outdoors again.

Corporal punishment may have worked like a gem on you, but spanking a defiant child will generally backfire.

It will generally cause problems to multiply rather than solving them. Once spanked, the strong-willed child usually will act out his intensified aggression on younger siblings, playmates, or schoolmates.

The older generation may disagree with this assessment. Your parents may ask, "What's this 'Time Out' stuff? We just got the hairbrush out and beat ya. What's wrong with that these days?" The answer is this: There are more effective ways to improve behavior, and we will discuss those in the final two sections of this book.

Myth: These Kids Don't Have the Skills to Behave

In the early 1980s, a lanky high school junior in North Carolina was told that he did not have enough basketball skill to wear a junior varsity uniform. He promptly went to the playgrounds around town and learned those skills. Two years later, he led the University of North Carolina to the NCAA Championship. After that, although his junior varsity skipper had told him that he lacked skill, Michael Jordan proved that he was talented enough to lead the Chicago Bulls to six NBA titles.

It may be tempting to point your finger at this infamous JV coach and call him an imbecile. But if you have ever believed that your defiant child did not have enough behavioral skills to understand right from wrong, you have fallen into exactly the same trap that the coach did.

As psychologists, we see many parents who worry that their kids don't have the skills to behave or socialize properly. Once we get to know these children, though, we find out that they are often loaded with skills. Without proper motivation, however, they won't use them.

One defiant child Ray counseled was a perfect example of this. His parents were convinced that low self-esteem contributed to his misbehavior, and that his low self-esteem was caused by a lack of social skills.

In reality, he had more friends than he knew what to do with. He could have taught a course on social skills. He just didn't choose to display them in front of his parents. Defiant kids often already have the skills; they just need to practice them more.

This said, some kids—the ones we've labeled "inflexible children"— do actually lack social skills. They have trouble figuring out what their parents want. They can pretty much tell what you don't want after receiving a few negative consequences. But when asked what they were supposed to do instead, they usually respond with vague comments such as "be good" or "behave," and they can't give you specific details because they don't have a clear idea of what they should do instead.

While we do work with some children who honest-to-goodness just don't have the skills, we refuse to excuse the many who actually do have the skills. All that most of these kids need is more teaching and more guidance. Just because they are lacking some skills doesn't mean that they can't behave. It just means that they will need more assistance in figuring out how to behave. That is where "Academies"— which we discuss in Chapter 20—come in so handy.

Myth: Children Must Fully Understand the Consequence Beforehand

A mother of three boys, Jenny felt like a nag. Her sons were addicted to Nintendo, and they needed at least five or six loud reminders to stop playing when dinnertime rolled around.

Bill's solution: Call the boys once. If they don't come down, they forfeit their right to a regular dinner. They may have only salads or something else nutritious, which they may not prefer.

When she heard this idea, Jenny immediately voiced a few myths. "But don't I need to tell them exactly how severe this consequence is going to be? And isn't it cruel to withhold food? Won't they starve to death?"

Jenny's fears are common among parents these days. But the truth is, you don't have to explain in excruciating detail what the consequences of an action are going to be. All you must do is let your child know that there will be consequences.

Actions speak louder than words, and Jenny's misbehaving boys won't understand how serious an empty stomach is until they experience it. They won't starve to death on vegetables or salad, but they will think twice before ignoring their mother when she calls them to dinner next time. We guarantee that they'll make up for the food shortage at breakfast the next morning.

Myth: My Kid Just Needs to Release His Anger— He Has Low Self-Esteem

One common belief is that children who lash out with their words or actions are simply venting their anger, and that their anger results from low self-esteem. According to this rationale, if children with low self-esteem vent their ill feelings, they'll be able to move on and their problems will magically disappear.

If you have ever been tempted to buy into this theory, it is not our point to shoot you down. This is a common misconception, one that is often shared with us by parents earnestly searching for help with a defiant child. They might bring the child in, announce to one of us that the boy is misbehaving because he has low self-esteem, and ask whether we would mind letting the boy vent for an hour or so during our scheduled therapy sessions. These parents honestly believe that their children will be fine if they can just release pent-up rage and frustration or find out what they are angry about. While that would be easy money for us, we both refuse to take parents up on that offer because we know that there are far more effective ways to improve kids' behavior.

Some therapists claim that angry behavior is an expression of a child's depression and that allowing the child to yell, scream, and cuss magically relieves some "pressure" so he won't blow up at home. It is entirely possible that your young child is depressed and feels bad about himself. He may very well act strong-willed in response to his feelings—we're not saying that this never happens among depressed children.

But an expression of anger alone is not automatically an indication of depression. Nor does it mean that your child is expressing low self-esteem if he throws asparagus spears at the family cat. It may not even mean that there is some deep, unresolved issue. Also, allowing a child to vent his feelings does not mean that bright and shiny days are ahead.

These kids sometimes do and sometimes don't have self-esteem issues or depression. You can't automatically assume that misbehavior is triggered by that—or that allowing your child to be rude and explosive is a good treatment for the problem.

Myth: His Medications Just Need to Be Increased

When a child's misbehavior increases, it is often easier for parents to wonder if there is something wrong with the child instead of contemplating what part they play in the problem. Too often, when a child on medication misbehaves, parents and therapists gravitate toward the simple solution that he needs more medicine—if for no other reason than that people tend to think that medication and "wonder drugs" are the answer to all woes.

Sometimes, more medication helps. Many times, it doesn't.

Frequently, defiant children misbehave not due to a low level of meds but because they figure that they can get away with it. Consider Kyle: He was talking out of turn and being the class clown in his last class of the day. His teacher immediately thought that his medication was wearing off and that he just needed more.

When Ray got involved in the case, he asked the teacher to try a new strategy: Instead of giving Kyle repeated warnings and putting his name on the board when he started acting up, the teacher was to send Kyle to the office. Once Kyle reached the office, the staff would call his mother to come and get him. Mom, who had been forewarned, would take him home and put him in his room. He could talk all he wanted in his room, but he had to remain there until 20 minutes after school let out (when he normally would arrive home). The teacher used this approach 2 days in a row. After that, miraculously, Kyle decided to sit quietly in his last period.

BEHAVIOR BASICS

Six Myths That Hamper Approaches to Managing Defiant Kids

1. *Myth: Nothing works with these kids.* The truth is that defiant children can be helped. Falling for this myth just hampers your ability to help your child.
2. *Myth: What these kids need is a good whop.* The truth is that spanking a defiant child encourages him to act out aggression on other children.
3. *Myth: These kids don't have the necessary skills to behave or cooperate.* The truth is that many of these kids have all the skills they need; they just don't choose to use them around you unless they're required to.
4. *Myth: Children must fully understand the consequence beforehand.* The truth is that consequences are an effective way to change behavior, regardless of whether the child knows exactly what's in store. All he needs to understand is that if he misbehaves, he'll have to pay a price.
5. *Myth: These are angry kids with low self-esteem, and they need to get their anger out to get better.* The truth is that there are better ways to help a defiant child than letting him scream.
6. *Myth: It's all biochemical.* The truth is that it's often *not* a lack of medication that is causing bad behavior. The child will change on his own if he is motivated to change.

His teacher was amazed that more medication was not required. Too often, though, we jump to the conclusion that medication is the best cure. It is always safest to use behavioral measures before resorting to medical means.

3

Getting the Monkey
off Your Back

Parents often say, "We're trying to improve his behavior, but he's not doing his part." Well, why should he? If a child doesn't feel the consequences of his behavior, he's not motivated to change.

This third section focuses on letting kids feel those consequences, and it shows you how to come up with consequences that work. We cannot overstress the importance of taking this step. A defiant child doesn't learn as well (or at all) from lectures or appeals to reason. He doesn't learn if you let him off the hook when he misbehaves because you feel sorry for him. But once you stop trying to cushion him from the consequences of his misbehavior, he will begin to be motivated to solve the problem.

Mentally prepare yourself for some of the toughest struggles you'll ever have.

Yes, it's going to be tough.

Yes, at times it may even feel impossible.

But oh, the rewards: Peace at the dinner table. Calm in the classroom. Quiet on Saturday afternoons. (Well, most of them, anyway.)

Sound good?

Turn the page.

It's His Head, Not Yours

How to Change Your Child from the
Problem into the Problem Solver

*I*n the days of milk trucks and Mickey Mantle, a young child of about 3 was obsessed with his father's milk truck. His father would even let him ride along every now and then when he made deliveries. While riding in it, the youngster could see the world passing swiftly by since the truck's doorways were wide open.

This child, whom we will call Jerry, thought that riding around with his dad was terrific. He loved making the rounds and, with his childish, broken vocabulary, he would occasionally request a seat on the truck by asking his father, "Go truck?"

One morning, he pulled up into his dad's lap at the breakfast table and asked, "Go truck?"

"No, son. I'm sorry, but I just don't have the time today," the father replied.

The youngster became agitated. He could not understand why

there was not enough time. In an angrier tone than before, Jerry bellowed, "Go truck!"

His father answered calmly but firmly, "Honey, we don't have time today. Maybe tomorrow. I'll look into seeing if you can go with me then. I'm sorry, but today is just not a good day."

Jerry launched on a tirade, shouting over and over, "Go *truck! Go truck!*" His father remained firm. At that point, Jerry jumped down and turned toward a brick fireplace. Picking up some momentum by running as fast as his 3-year-old legs could carry him, he smashed his head on the brick wall. The impact cut his head wide open, and it bled profusely, as scalp injuries in children often do. His mother scooped him off the floor, flew her car to the hospital, and had his head stitched up. He returned home with 4 inches of bandage wrapped around his noggin and a headache that would not quit until he fell asleep that night.

The next day, still wearing the pillowlike bandage, Jerry turned to his father and asked, "Go truck?"

"No, son, I can't do it today," said the father. "You can't go today, but thanks."

"Go truck!" said Jerry.

"No," replied his father.

Enraged, Jerry looked at his father, looked at the wall, and looked back again at his dad with a gleam in his eye. After this threatening little gesture, he said menacingly, "Go truck." His father replied, "It's your head," then walked out the door to run his rounds. He got in his truck and drove off.

As you might guess, Jerry didn't make a mad dash at that wall; he'd quickly figured out that he wasn't going to get his way even if he did. And he'd already learned that the wall was tougher than his head.

In therapy, we encourage parents to pull back, as Jerry's father did, so that their defiant children can feel the consequences of their own decisions. When a child learns that Mom and Dad aren't going to make everything right if he does something wrong, he will begin thinking: "Uh-oh. This is not good. I need to do something different."

This is a beginning. This is where children start to develop their ability to think for themselves and to solve problems on their own. And this way, children get to experience consequences at a younger age. Simply put: It is better for your child to fall and scrape his knees while learning to ride a bike than to run into a tree while learning to drive a car.

Although teaching defiant kids with consequences is hard, it *does* work. And it is the only way to get through to them. We encourage you to let your defiant child experience as many consequences as possible so he can see that the consequences are stronger than he is.

Divorce Yourself from the Problem, Not the Child

You may have heard about the gardener tending to his flowers who noticed some frantic activity in a nearby cocoon. Upon further investigation, he discovered that a butterfly was trying to emerge from the strong, white fabric. The gardener fumbled around in his pocket for a pocketknife, which he used to carve out a hole big enough for the butterfly to climb through. Moments after the multicolored bug climbed out onto the gardener's hand, its wings crumpled together and it fell dead on its side.

There were no fatal bacteria on the man's hand, and he hadn't accidentally wounded the butterfly with his knife. The butterfly died because it needed the natural struggle of fighting through the cocoon to strengthen its majestic wings to fly. Without the labor that God intended it to experience, the butterfly was unable to grow strong enough to soar above the garden on a lazy spring day.

Like that gardener, parents are often tempted to carry their defiant children over one hurdle and set them on solid ground—where sooner or later they will need help clearing another obstacle. The result is much like with the butterfly: The kids never grow strong enough to handle their own problems.

The best way to work with a defiant child is to care for him but not get involved in solving his problems. We advise you to pretend that your child is actually a friend of his who has come over to visit. Parents often say that they get along fine with their children's friends. They enjoy them, they talk openly, and, importantly, their advice is tempered and sparse.

For example, when your child's buddy plops down at your kitchen table and begins to complain about all his woes—like the discipline that he's received at home or at school—you don't feel compelled to save him from his despair. Instead, you may unwittingly display attributes of love, but you won't solve the problem.

The youngster might say, "You know, my mom is so mean. She makes me take out the garbage every single day, and she makes me clean up my room, and I'm supposed to be on summer vacation."

The way you might handle it would be to momentarily stop preparing dinner, sincerely gaze in his direction, and say, "Oh, Johnny, that is so terrible." At that moment, you are caring, concerned, and polite. You are listening to him, understanding what he is saying, and talking to him with warmth and empathy. But the key point is that you are not overinvolved.

The youngster can tell that you understand how he feels. You have acknowledged him and allowed him to feel good about your relationship with him, and at the same time you have allowed him to retain his problem without taking it on yourself. Once your child's friend has said his spiel, or once dinner is ready, you kindly send the child back home so you can feed your family their supper in peace.

This is emotionally divorcing yourself from the child's problem without divorcing yourself from the child. Put another way, this tactic allows you to be loving without being overinvolved or being underinvolved, neither of which shows love or solves the problem. Granted, you may find it difficult to separate yourself from emotional involvement when it's your kid who has run into some trouble, but if you intervene, you'll do more harm than good. You'll take away his opportunity to learn and grow.

The Dangers of Overinvolvement

Being overinvolved puts you in the same category as the good-hearted gardener who unintentionally killed a lovely butterfly. By smothering your child and solving his problems, you prevent him from developing wisdom through experience. You take away the opportunity to learn one of the grandest lessons ever. No one would like that. It is just not fair.

You may think that you're making life easier on your kid if you complete the vast majority of his school projects for him, but you are really hurting him because later in life he will not have the basic skills he needs to complete a project for his employer.

There is danger in not letting children solve their own problems. It's also risky to prevent their problems and to save them from feeling discomfort for a time. Children who are protected by overinvolved parents will one day learn that they are not as competent as they thought, and they will discover that they are not capable of solving their own problems. This translates into a feeling of helplessness and will likely lead to depression and low self-esteem.

The Problems with Underinvolvement

We'll give you a worst-case example of truly being self-centered and underinvolved: Several years ago, some parents in Chicago left their two small children alone at home over Christmas break while they went to Acapulco for their own vacation. Not only were they meeting their own needs at their children's expense, but they were also neglecting their children and exhibiting poor parenting skills.

We know that you care about your child and we doubt that the thought of doing something as blatantly noncaring as that has ever seriously crossed your mind. But there are degrees of underinvolvement.

Something that might hit a little closer to home is a working mother who felt too busy to spend "quantity time" with her two children. A highly successful businesswoman, this lady poured all her energy into her job, regularly working 45 to 55 hours per week. She rarely came home before her kids' bedtime on weekdays, and when she was home during waking hours, she pushed her children away, claiming that she needed "quiet time" after a long day's work. When weekends would roll around, she would leave the house for a massage or some other self-indulging treat. "I work hard all week. I deserve to have weekends to myself," she would often say to her husband.

Meanwhile, her husband did spend time with the kids. But the children, starved for attention from their mother, misbehaved badly—especially when Mom was around.

During a therapy session with Bill, the father traced the history of his marriage to this workaholic, self-centered lady. He said that before they had kids, he spent much of his attention on her. Rather than reciprocating, she also tended to her needs. Once the children entered their lives, he began to shift much of his time and energy to caring for his kids. But his wife continued to focus on herself. And her underinvolvement was sparking all kinds of reckless misbehavior from her children, who craved just a moment or two of her attention.

Though this may be an extreme example, we urge you to take a good look at your priorities. We know how worn out you may feel after a long week of work, with the boss demanding more and coworkers finding flaws in your efforts. But that is not an excuse to deprive your kids of the love and attention they need and deserve. During the workweek, save as much gusto for your child or children as possible. Not only will your involvement improve their behavior, you'll also feel a closer bond with the most important people in your life: your family.

Revisiting the Brick Wall

Just before Bill's father died from cancer, he came down to visit Bill in Arizona, where Bill was living at the time. They started talking and the elder O'Hanlon began reflecting on his life in a casual conversation. He said that he had learned one thing, a most valuable lesson, from raising eight kids.

That got Bill's curiosity going. What was the one thing he had learned? Bill's mind became a tape recorder as his father began to speak:

"What I learned is that each of my kids has to hit a brick wall, and that is how they learn about life. I went through several different phases in trying to help you kids avoid the brick wall, but I finally learned that you had to hit it on your own to find out it was there. Eventually, you learned that I knew what I was talking about."

He said that his first two children's learning experiences started out like this:

Metaphorically, one of his kids would be heading for trouble—riding a motorcycle aimed for a brick wall. As a parent, the elder O'Hanlon could see the brick wall. He would step off the curb, stand between his kid and the wall, flail his arms like an airport's pilot guide, and yell something like "Hey, you're headed for a brick wall. You're about to mess up with that drinking. You're getting bad grades at school and won't be able to go on to college. You're involved with someone who is clearly taking advantage of you and will break your heart."

His kid would then give a defiant response, rev up the motorcycle, gesture rudely at him, and crash headlong into him—and then the wall.

"We both would hit the brick wall, and we were both damaged pretty badly," he recalled of his early attempts at raising children.

After getting sandwiched between the hypothetical motorcycle and the emotional brick wall many times with his first two kids, Mr. O'Hanlon wised up a bit. Rather than stepping off the curb, he held his perch on the street's edge and loudly warned the next several children. This method produced the same result—minus the serious damage to the father. The kids still sped up, gestured rebelliously, and pounded into the brick wall.

Finally, after watching six children slam into countless brick walls, Mr. O'Hanlon got the message.

"I realized, 'Oh, this is how kids learn,'" he said. "After that, I would take a seat on a curbside bench and tell my youngest two kids, 'Look. I'm an old man. I've been around for a while. I think there is a brick wall up there. I think you're headed for it. You probably think I'm full of it, and you probably won't listen because you think you know better than I. Here is your opportunity to learn whether you do or not.' When I'd say it that way, they would slow down, the rude gesture would drop out, but they would still hit the brick wall. That is the way kids learn that there are limits in life, that there are consequences, and that they are accountable for what they do afterward.

"You know, it never got any easier to see my kids hit the brick wall. I always wanted them not to hit the brick wall. I finally just realized that they all would, in one way or another. Sometimes, it would tear my heart out. If I thought they were going to die, I would reach over and try to pull the key out of the motorcycle—but only if it was going to be a fatal consequence. If they intended to go drinking and driving, Dad got the key.

"Now, you can't follow them around every minute, but if you know they are messing up in big ways, you have to take more stringent action. Generally, they have to hit brick walls, and that is how kids learn about life and who is responsible."

This message from Bill's dad is a key to this whole book. *Experience is a child's best teacher.* A lot of parents visit therapists like us not because their kids are doing something pathological or sick or wrong or out of the ordinary, but because the parents are uncomfortable with their child's natural learning process and do not want to tolerate the discomfort.

It's just like the kindly gardener, who would have found it difficult to sit back and watch the butterfly struggle.

Imagine how beautiful the butterfly would have looked fluttering through the fresh roses and daisies if the gardener hadn't tried to help. As parents, we can enjoy a similar vision when we let our children work their way through the tough fabric of their own personal cocoons.

Microwave Wisdom

Everything is getting faster-paced these days. We have high-speed tape recorders, gigabyte computers, and even 75-mile-an-hour speed limits in some states. As so many other things speed up to make lives easier, parents may be tempted to find ways to accelerate the pace at which their children mature.

But this is where technology hits a snag. People must experience valleys to appreciate the mountain peaks. We humans must struggle with our shoelaces for hours before lacing up becomes a nonthinking process. Part of wisdom is going through experiences and savoring them. This concept is true for both your child and you.

You may be wondering, "What if I screw up? What if I really mess up?"

Our answer to this is simple: "Hey, even if you fall flat on your face, at least you will be headed in the right direction."

One of the biggest issues we see among parents is that they want to inject their wisdom into their children with the same speed that a polio vaccine enters the bloodstream. As nice as that idea sounds, parents must realize that kids *cannot* gain wisdom that way. There is only one method that works: trial-and-error experiences over a long period of time.

Just as in the story about Bill's father and the brick wall, there are times when you'll have to remove the key from the motorcycle. But for most kids, the risk of severe injury is lower at younger ages, so it's acceptable to let them slowly learn with each stumble.

At age 8, a child will usually only skin his knee or bruise his arm when his hypothetical motorcycle slams into the "wall." At age 12, his injury might require stitches or even a cast to heal a broken bone. But if your child isn't allowed to hit the brick wall until he's 18 or older, he'll have picked up enough speed on that motorcycle to knock himself into a coma or, possibly, death.

The later you wait to let your child discover the consequences of his actions, the more likely he is to set up patterns that will mess him up worse in the future.

The Value of Trial and Error

In therapy, our objective is to set up brick wall scenarios in which children are likely to find their noses planted in red brick and mortar. This may sound cruel. You may be thinking, "What a nasty pair of therapists. I can't believe I supported you guys by buying this book." You must understand that we don't put kids in dangerous situations; we just give them opportunities to learn.

Take, for example, the first time that Ray was exposed to this concept. When Ray was 9 years old and living in Richmond, Virginia, his mother took him on a flight to visit his grandmother in Boston. While at the airport, his mother decided to give Ray an opportunity to learn on his own.

Ray's grandmother was getting up in years and could barely hear or see. Ray's mother told him to pretend that *she* was his grandmother and asked him to lead her to the right gate. She tucked her arm under Ray's elbow, and the knobby-kneed youngster—who would one day earn a degree from Harvard—twice escorted his mother past, not through, the correct gate at a changeover in New York's La Guardia Airport.

Mother Levy gave no indication to Ray that he'd messed up. Finally, something clicked in young Ray's mind and he realized precisely where the correct gate was. He led his mother there, and they arrived with only seconds to spare.

Years later, Ray asked his mother why she hadn't intervened and why she instead risked paying a steep fee to catch a later flight. "It would have cost you $100 to get us on a later flight if we'd missed that one," Ray said. "Why didn't you just tell me where we were supposed to go?"

His mother leaned back in her recliner and said with a knowing smile, "Oh, we would have figured something out."

Ray's mother realized the value of letting him learn in a controlled environment.

Parents and teachers commonly ask us to help their children develop better "coping skills" or "problem-solving skills." These adults believe that we possess some magical power for talking to their children. They think that we can snap our fingers and help the child "realize" his coping skills, or that we can put him in a "problem-solving skills class" and miraculously give the child skills that he hasn't yet learned in school.

You don't need to resort to magic to help a child truly grasp these skills. He simply must experience a need for the skills. This only occurs when a child experiences uncomfortable situations and chooses to act or react differently next time. Once he experiences a need, he can become quite creative in solving the problem. All adults can do is provide children with opportunities.

Taping pillows on children's knees when they learn to skate is nice because it prevents them from scraping their knees when they fall. But it will also prevent them from ever learning how to skate well. Children have to fall. That is part of learning how to skate. That's why the brick wall story is so vital in explaining this concept: It lets parents know that

BEHAVIOR BASICS

The Brick Wall Strategy: Helping Children Learn through Experience

▶ Don't try to instill wisdom in your child or prevent him from feeling the consequences of his actions. He must experience how the world works before he can attain his own wisdom.

▶ Emotionally divorce yourself from the problem, not the child. This forces him to solve his own problem.

▶ Let your child know that his feelings are valid and that you are sad when he experiences things that are uncomfortable or painful.

▶ Don't try to buffer your child from discomfort or painful learning experiences. He needs to *feel* life to learn from it.

this is how their children learn. It is not a fun process. It takes up a lot of time. It is not always easy, and it often breaks your heart.

But it is necessary.

Normally, trial and error hurts the parent longer than it hurts the child. When kids bang their heads into a wall, we parents may still be feeling the pain inside while our kids are back on their bikes—laughing and learning.

9

Avoiding a Power Struggle

Five Rules *You* Should Learn
to Help Your Child Learn

B illy was aggressive, disrespectful, and rude toward his classmates and teachers. One day, he aggressively grabbed a ball from another child and ran away with it. When his teacher approached Billy, the young boy told her precisely what had happened, why his behaviors were inappropriate, and what he should have done instead.

This frustrated his teacher to no end. Billy knew how to behave appropriately, but he refused to. In fact, Billy had already visited several well-respected psychologists and graduated from two social skills courses. Unsure of what to do next, Billy's teacher approached Ray about this case. Why, the teacher wanted to know, had Billy not turned the corner after all this training?

The reason was simple: *Billy just was not inspired.*

He understood exactly what he was supposed to do in specific situations; he just chose not to do the right thing.

Billy's case was such a revelation for Ray that it encouraged him to alter his entire practice. Like most child therapists at the time, Ray had been trying to change defiant behavior by training the defiant child. But that direction often doesn't work because the child is the least motivated person in any defiant situation. As Ray learned, if you want to make a child less defiant, you (the adult) have to concentrate on improving the situation because as a parent, teacher, or counselor you are much more motivated than the child is.

After reflecting on Billy's case for a while, Ray switched the focus of his therapy program from children to adults. In the 10 years since that switch, the successes have grown dramatically.

In perfecting his adult training therapy, Ray has discovered that there are five key rules that you should follow to start helping your child improve—much as Billy did, once his teacher took the initiative rather than waiting for him to do so.

1. To shut down arguments, say little or nothing.
2. If your child tries to manipulate you, respond with brain-dead phrases.
3. Douse your child's fire with your sadness; don't fuel it with your anger.
4. Recognize that offering more choices can reduce power struggles.
5. Never tell a child what he's just learned.

Rule #1: Zip It or Clip It

So often, defiant children make inappropriate decisions that create hassles for others. Usually, when this happens, most adults want to launch into a lecture. Either they believe that their words of wisdom will dramatically alter the kids' perspectives and faults or they just want to vent their feelings.

If it makes you feel better to talk, go for it. But don't expect your words to have any positive effect on your difficult child. In fact, they may very well have a negative effect.

A defiant child learns almost exclusively from his own experiences and the consequences of his own actions—not from hearing about yours. This trait makes him a pioneer for tomorrow. (Unfortunately, it makes him a pain in the butt for you today.)

Lecturing not only does no good, it also helps your child think that he is winning the struggle. The best thing that you can do when your child makes a bad choice is to give a consequence and then be quiet. That's what we mean by "Zip it."

For example, after you tell a misbehaving child that he can't play video games for the rest of the day, you may feel like rubbing it in a little: "If you'd just have turned the volume down when I asked you 5 minutes ago, you could have played to your heart's content." Don't. Instead, Zip It. If you must speak, say something like, "Sorry about your computer games, son." Then move on. This way, your child's mind is free to focus on solving the problem rather than struggling with you.

Believe us, we know this is hard. Our tongues bear teeth marks from forcing ourselves to hold back words. But this strategy is what works best with a defiant child. We've seen too many parents and teachers become absolutely flustered when a child does not respond to their well-intentioned lectures. It's almost as if they expect these defiant children to listen intently and say, "You know, what you said has a lot of merit to it. I've never really thought about it that way. I really appreciate your sharing your great wisdom, and I will now correct my wrongful ways. Thank you so much for sharing."

Although we'd all like our lectures to affect children this way, most of us will never experience anything remotely similar. So, we all just need to stop trying! Your child will develop better coping skills if you can Zip It and just stay quiet.

Even tougher is not responding when your child makes provocative statements, which often seem to be for the sole purpose of annoying you. Defiant kids will often make statements like "You love my little brother more than me!". . . "You're the meanest mom in the world!". . . "Johnny told me to steal it!". . . "Bobby told me to hit him!". . . "If you don't buy me a new car, I'll be embarrassed in front of all my friends, and that will hurt my self-esteem!". . . and other poignant statements that beckon you to respond with venom.

In these situations, if you absolutely feel compelled to say something, Clip It. By that we mean make your statement short, sweet, and to the point, and get out of there as soon as possible. (We'll talk more about this technique in the next section.)

When you respond with either the Zip It or the Clip It technique, your child will be thrown entirely off base. Without you to argue with, he is much like a tennis player whose opponent has walked off the court: He has to find another game to play. And as a last resort, your child will be forced to think. He'll have to figure out whether he wants to continue with his misbehavior and deal with the consequences, or modify his strategy and game.

We can't always assure you that your child will change his strategy. But we can assure you that if you repeatedly lecture and respond with anger, you will only keep him set in his ways.

Rule #2: Use Brain-Dead Phrases

Brain-dead phrases are comments you can use to let your child know that you're not going to engage in any of his ridiculous arguing or silly questioning. These expressions affect your child more than simply ignoring him does because disregarding things that bug us is not something that most humans do very easily. (Even though we commonly recommend it to our children, we've never mastered it.)

One of our favorite brain-dead phrases is "I understand," which is delivered with sadness in your voice. When your child says, "That's not fair! This really sucks," all you have to say is "I understand." No more, no less. Or, if your defiant student says, "Last week, Suzy talked in class and you didn't make her stay in during recess," you can substitute the words "Could be."

We recommend that adults choose several brain-dead phrases off the list on pages 70–71. After a while, you can expand that number if you choose. You could start out with "I know," and then use "Thanks for letting me know how you are thinking about this." Children often make provocative statements as a way to enrage parents or adults. Their goal in doing that is to derail you and to avoid a consequence. When that happens, thanking the child works well and helps you stay on track.

For instance, Bill was once in a therapy session with a father and

(continued on page 72)

Brain-Dead Phrases You Can Use

Children will normally and naturally try to avoid the consequences of their actions by manipulating their parents or teachers. This is a normal developmental process and does not mean that anything is wrong with the child.

This said, defiant children are more manipulating than others, especially if they find you an easy target. The best way to avoid being manipulated is to respond with a brain-dead phrase.

Below are some common ways that children hook parents and some brain-dead phrases that will short-circuit the manipulation. Please note: The same phrase can be used in different situations.

1. Child disputes the facts.
   CHILD: *"I was only in 30 minutes late!"* [child actually missed curfew by 2 hours]
   PARENT (CALMLY AND WITH A SMILE): *"Good try."*
2. Child challenges a rule.
   CHILD: *"Time Out doesn't work; it's stupid."*
   PARENT (IN A MATTER-OF-FACT TONE): *"Could be."*
3. Child adamantly claims that he was not responsible for his behavior.
   CHILD (AFTER HITTING YOU IN A FIT OF RAGE): *"It was your fault that I hit you because you made me mad."*
   PARENT (WITH SADNESS): *"Sorry you feel that way."* [Parent then administers the consequences anyway.]
4. Child argues about the fairness of a rule or consequence.
   CHILD: *"That's not fair; I shouldn't be grounded for a week; I just missed one assignment."*
   PARENT (WITH SADNESS): *"I understand."* [Remember, understanding doesn't mean agreement.]
5. Child personally attacks a quality of your parenting.
   (a) Your intentions
   CHILD: *"You're mean and you're just a power junkie and you're just doing this because it makes you feel good."*

PARENT: *"Thanks for letting me know how you are thinking about this."*

(b) Love/devotion

CHILD: *"You wouldn't do this to Michael; you love him more than you do me."*

PARENT: *"Sorry you feel that way . . . hope you get over it real soon."*

(c) Values

CHILD: *"You're cheap; that's why you won't buy me that video game."*

PARENT (WITH A SMILE): *"Good try."*

6. Child tries to bargain or negotiates about the consequences.

CHILD: *"Okay, I'll take the grounding, but not this weekend because I have tickets already for the Third Eye Blind concert. I'll stay in next weekend."*

PARENT: *"Good effort. Wouldn't it be nice if that worked?"*

7. Child attempts to use terrorism to get you to give in.

CHILD: *"If you take my phone line out then I'll run away."*

PARENT (CALMLY): *"Sorry that you feel that you have to resort to that."* [Parent then breaks eye contact and walks away. Never negotiate with a terrorist.]

8. Child refuses to obey an instruction.

CHILD: *"I'll clean up my room when I feel like it."*

PARENT (CALMLY): *"Wish that worked."* [Parent then backs off and enforces a consequence later, when the child wants to do something he enjoys.]

Remember that when you use a brain-dead phrase, you must say it with sadness or indifference but never with anger or sarcasm, since that will only encourage your child to struggle with you.

child. The child told Bill that he thought it was all right for a person to carry a gun in his car in case anyone hassled him on the road. That way, the child reasoned, the driver could defend himself and shoot the other person. At that point, the father looked desperately at Bill and said, "He can't think that way. You've got to make him stop thinking like that. One of these days, he's going to get himself killed."

Rather than appearing rattled, Bill calmly looked at the youngster and said, "Thanks for letting us know how you are thinking about that." The child was silenced. He began to realize that he couldn't get under Bill's skin and rattle him as he had his father.

Another response that we recommend for parents is "Good try!" This phrase should be delivered with a little smile on your face. It works well when your child comes up with some ridiculous argument attempting to make you defend your position. For example, let's say that your child fibs and tells you that he wasn't late for class. He says that the teacher mistakenly gave him the tardy slip thinking that he was someone else. "See, there's a kid in class who looks just like me," your child says. Rather than wasting your time and energy on this petty argument, the best thing to do is smile and say "Good try!" The message you are giving is: "Gee, wouldn't that be nice if it worked? Unfortunately, it doesn't."

The last brain-dead phrase that we recommend is "Wish that worked," stated with a flat tone. You want to use this when your child is in his "try and make me" mode. You ask the child to do something, he refuses, and you reply with "Wish that worked." That means to your child, "Wish that worked for you, because it definitely won't work for me, and there will be a consequence later."

Here's how this phrase worked with Jared, a 14-year-old who was sitting at the dinner table with his siblings and father. Jared was being rude to his siblings, so his father said, "Jared, this is not a fun meal for us. I want you to leave the table and go eat somewhere else." Jared looked up defiantly and spouted out, "I'm not leaving, and you can't make me." With a relaxed tone in his voice, the father said, "Wish that worked." Translation: "Don't worry about it, Jared. There will be a consequence later on. We'll take care of this after a while. And we'll do it on my time."

Jared didn't get up from the table, but he also did not get a ride to basketball practice that night. The next weekend, he also didn't get to stay overnight with a friend. When he complained, his father replied, "Look, honey, I don't do nice things for people who don't do nice things for me and who disobey the rules of this house. But I will get over it. Why don't you ask me for something some other time?"

The next time Jared misbehaved at the dinner table, Dad asked him to leave. This time, Jared left willingly. Before long, he stopped acting up at dinner altogether.

There are many other brain-dead phrases you can use, but the object is not to use as many as you can. The point is to avoid unnecessary struggles with your child. These phrases work beautifully with strong-willed kids because you are using brief statements rather than changing the color of your face and the tone of your voice in an argument. You are *reacting* differently. That takes the fun out of arguing with you.

Rule #3: Cool It

Few things are more inviting for strong-willed children than to be able to get your goat. They find controlling your emotions, expressions, and actions invigorating and reinforcing. It's probably more effective than beckoning them with M&M's.

Yet, as parents, most of us just don't get this fact. We tend to yell, scream, nag, and cajole, expecting our kids to change just from the power of our bluster. That's not the way it works.

Anger toward defiant kids is like lighter fluid on a fire. The more anger you throw at them, the more they feed off of it. When you stop throwing lighter fluid on it, a fire eventually dies out. When you stop using anger to try to control your defiant child, his attempts to control you in that fashion will eventually cease.

So if you want your child to change, quit feeding him your anger, which he wants and enjoys. Instead, give him what he doesn't want: your sadness or understanding.

We don't mean that you will actually feel pangs of compassion for your child; we're just recommending that you come across as sad when your child earns a consequence for bad behavior. When you appear saddened, it automatically blocks the anger that children normally feel toward you after they have made a bad choice.

For example, if your child earns a consequence such as missing out on a party after busting curfew the week before, don't angrily lecture him. Respond with sadness—as though you'd rather that the punishment not happen. In this way, you have unloaded the struggle onto your child alone, so it is no longer between you and him.

If you respond with sadness, your child is more likely to learn the lesson from his consequence. He won't grow upset with you or get distracted by defending his right to make mistakes and decide for himself.

Several years ago, Ray tried this approach during a summer vacation with his family in Colorado. Rachel, his daughter, wanted to walk barefoot outside the hotel. He immediately argued and told her to get those Nikes on her feet before she got a splinter. She refused, saying that she wanted to be like Pocahontas. After a few minutes of intense debate, Ray realized that a child psychologist was losing an argument with his then-4-year-old daughter. So he threw up his hands and said, "Fine, go barefoot."

Within 50 feet of the hotel room, Rachel yelped, drew her foot up, and began screaming for her mommy. She had stepped on a little shard of glass, and her foot was bleeding slightly. The first thought that popped into Ray's head was to get angry, point at her, and say, "See! I told you so!" Instead, he bit his tongue and said, "Oh, honey! That must hurt. Let Daddy pick you up, and we'll go get that bandaged up."

That was not an easy response for Ray. Child psychologists aren't superparents. They experience the same urges as everyone else. But resisting that temptation to say "I told you so!" is critical. If he had reacted with anger, Rachel could have made comments like "It doesn't hurt!" or "Who put that glass there? It must have been a bad man." By responding with sadness, Ray let her think through the consequence.

She never pulled the Pocahontas routine again. She did, however, decide to go out one day without wearing her socks. But she learned very quickly what happens when you walk around the mall with no socks. The blisters eventually went away, but the lesson is in her mind to stay.

We know that you're not going to automatically feel like

responding with sadness to your child's inappropriate behavior. It's not natural to respond this way, and it often goes against your parental instincts. But keep this in mind: We are not recommending that you *feel* differently, just that you *react* differently. If this seems hard to do, try practicing and preparing yourself in advance. Practice also helps you to appear genuine when the consequence must be passed out. We will talk more about these rehearsals in "Training Camp," Chapter 14.

Rule #4: More Choices Equal Fewer Struggles

For you physics majors, here is an equation: Choices equal control. That means that when you begin giving your child more choices, you'll notice that he instigates fewer and fewer control battles.

Many times, we dictate to our children what we want and expect. When we do that, we're often thrust into an unnecessary power struggle. But if we would simply toss a choice in with it—a choice that we as adults could live with—there would be fewer power struggles.

Ray once counseled a mother who had horrendous fights every day over how her 8-year-old girl's hair should be fixed. The mother came to therapy sessions immaculate. She was obsessive—not one hair out of place—and she was creating titanic power struggles by forcing her daughter to be just as picky. Mom was too concerned with what other people would think of her if her daughter did not look her best.

Ray said two things: One, other people often don't judge you by how your daughter looks; if they do, they're too superficial. And two, aren't you more interested in how your daughter views *you* than in what strangers think?

Realizing the truth in these questions, Mom began to focus on relaxing her standards. When she did, her relationship with her daughter became less adversarial and much more fun. She reported back to Ray that she and her daughter "haven't been this close since she was a newborn."

It was important that the mother give her daughter more control in how she looked—within reason. We firmly believe that kids should be able to dress as they want, except for formal events.

By giving your child choices, you allow him to do most of the thinking. You also hand him the keys to the "control" car—something that every kid wants. Giving up some control often will serve a second purpose as well: By modeling flexibility, you are being an example for your child. Many children will follow suit.

The Types of Choices Your Child Might Make

Many of you reading this will have your hands on your hips and say, "But my child will make the wrong choice, and that will cause me more hassle to clean up their mistakes." Our answer: Yep! This is how kids learn.

When Ray's daughter was 8 years old, he would often let her direct him in how to take her to school. The first day, she told him to take a right at the wrong stoplight. Pop and daughter went many miles out of the way. Rachel was lost. She finally found her way and directed Ray back to her school with no help from her father. Was Ray late for his appointments? Yes! Was Rachel late for school? Of course! But what Rachel learned about navigating through the streets of suburban Dallas was far more important than either of those inconveniences.

By giving as many choices as possible and allowing your child to make bad ones, you give your child a wonderful gift of learning and failing in a safe environment.

"Do you want to wash or dry the dishes?" is an appropriate choice for a child. Sure, sometimes your child may say "Neither." But when you give your kid power over the small things, he will be more likely to give in about the big things. When kids have a sense of control, they won't fight with you as much.

Here are some reasonable choices to offer at home: "Do you want to take a bath now or in 15 minutes?". . . "Do you want to make your bed before breakfast or after you eat your scrambled eggs?". . . "Do you want to go to bed at 8:30 or 8:45?"

And, when possible, give choices for meals: "Would you rather have peas or broccoli with your supper?"

At school, a teacher might offer these choices: "Do you want to complete this worksheet in pencil or pen?". . . "Would you rather have a break now or after you finish your math assignment?". . . "Would you rather do the even problems or the odd ones first?"

We often fail to give choices because we think that our way is the best way. We get into time crunches and forget to allow our kids some element of control. Yet every small choice you can give will help quench your child's thirst for control. A little time now can prevent a power struggle later.

Rule #5: Never Tell Children What They Just Learned

At one time or another, every parent has warned a child about the dangers of touching a hot stove. We tell them how excruciating the pain of a burn is, and we tell them how long it takes to heal. But sometimes, the kid still touches the stove, just so he can find out for himself. It is tempting—downright enticing—to say "I told you so!" while the child hops up and down and blows on his hands.

But those are four words you must never say.

Just as you have dignity and pride, your child has self-respect too. When you point out the lesson your child has just learned, you are squashing that dignity.

Kids who have been told the lesson that they just learned will often turn right around and do almost the exact same thing again as a way to "show" you. They are trying to save face and let you know that they can learn their own lessons, thank you very much.

Bill once had an 11-year-old client who tried to impress his father by hanging on the monkey bars and using a yo-yo at the same time. While the youngster was hanging, the yo-yo bounced up and popped him in the face. The father couldn't resist the opportunity to say "Well, that was stupid. I bet that hurt!"

Angered by his dad's remark, the son stopped crying, hung back down on the monkey bars, flipped the yo-yo down, and caught it with his forehead again. The 11-year-old knew exactly what was going to happen again, and he didn't care. He wanted to show his father that he could learn his own lessons.

A defiant kid doesn't want to listen and learn from your experiences; he wants to find out for himself. We've learned this from Bill's experience with the yo-yo child and from a quiz that Ray uses with almost every child he's ever seen in therapy. When a child completes therapy, Ray asks what was responsible for the change. For example, he'll remark, "Jackie, 6 weeks ago, you were giving your parents a hassle about getting up in the morning. Remember that?" Jackie nods his head. "You were also bugging your little sister at the breakfast table, and you were refusing to do your homework when you got home from school. You recall that as well?" Again Jackie's head bobs up and down affirmatively. "Well, what happened? Why did you change?"

Jackie answers the same as just about every other kid that Ray has ever had in his office—with a cocky air: "I just decided to."

Jackie—and every other youngster we've known who has changed—is saying that he will not give anyone else credit for the

BEHAVIOR BASICS

Shutting Down Power Struggles

Zip it. Allow your child to feel his consequence—resist the urge to tell him what he did wrong. If you must talk, clip it down to the bare minimum.

Use brain-dead phrases. Using these quick-hit lines with perseverance shows your child that you refuse to take responsibility for his behavior.

Cool it. When your child does something inappropriate, don't respond in anger. Just express your sadness as you give him the consequence. Sadness douses the fire; anger fuels it.

Recognize that more choices mean less struggle. Since control is what a defiant child wants, give it to him—within reason. Let him make choices fit for a child, such as whether to make the bed or brush his teeth first. This way, you're letting your child feel that he's in control.

Never say "I told you so." If your child gets hurt because he disobeyed you, don't rub his face in the fact that you were right. He can figure that out himself.

change that has occurred within him. Defiant kids need credit for their improvement. Each child must see himself as the sole instigator behind that change. Defiant kids are not willing to watch anyone else take credit when they learn an important lesson. To them, that would be giving away too much power.

Don't get us wrong. It would make any therapist's day for Jackie and all the other kids to walk into the office and thank us lavishly for helping them. But neither of us have ever had a young client do that, nor do we expect one to.

Neither should you. You can consider the increased peacefulness in your home as your reward.

If you follow these five basic rules, most defiant children soon become great problem solvers—just as they once were exceptional problem creators—because they won't get the *reaction* they want from you.

Some defiant children, however, will continue to push your limits. That doesn't mean that you need to panic; it just means that such a youngster needs further action from you. If your child still is not solving his own problems, he's probably just not motivated enough. At that point we need to up the ante, which is the focus of the next few chapters.

Upping the Ante by Intensifying the Positives

Ever wonder why you don't have your child's cooperation? It's simple: You haven't earned it.

That's right—*earned*.

Unlike when you were a kid, respect and cooperation are no longer automatic. If you want your child to follow your rules, you first have to gain his attention by developing a healthy relationship with him. Constantly criticizing him, no matter how accurate your remarks may be, won't build that relationship. Instead you'll just turn him off.

Think of it as a formula: *Rules without Relationship = Rebellion*.

To create a healthy bond with your defiant kiddo, you must first "up the ante" by using what we call "positives."

This next part of the book shows you how to use simple techniques and rules to avoid unnecessary power struggles while constructing a more solid relationship. Remember, without a strong connection, any of the negative consequences you impose will backfire into a cloud of rebellion.

So clear your mind of any negative thoughts and prepare yourself to focus on the positives.

Growing Your Relationship

How to Positively Motivate
Your Child

A wise mother once said, "You can attract more bees with honey than with vinegar." As we've walked through life these past fortysomething years, we've noticed that, as usual, Mom was right—and not just about the bees. This same philosophy is one we use with defiant kids. Criticism and negativity do not bring out the best in kids or anyone else. In fact, they generally do quite the opposite. Commenting *solely* on what a child does incorrectly not only gives him little direction on how to behave correctly, it also often brings out more defiance.

As we mentioned in Part 1, control is important to defiant children. These kids consider the negativity, criticism, and yelling that they receive from others as forms of their control over those people; that is, they feel as though they are pushing buttons on a remote control, causing adults to act a certain way. But the good news is that as much as they thrive on negativity, these kids like—and respond favorably to—positives. For these reasons, we recommend that you start with positives as a way to build a better relationship with your child.

Another reason that we suggest focusing on positives first is that parents of a defiant child often find themselves in a negative feedback loop. They tune in only to the negative actions of their child and overlook the small steps that the child is taking to improve.

We'll be honest: Negative behaviors are what most often stand out. Are you more likely to notice the child sitting quietly doing homework or the one flinging dishes in the kitchen? And defiant children give you ample opportunity to note their inappropriate behavior—they exhibit plenty of it, and they produce it frequently throughout the day. Naturally, this helps the negativity loop feed on itself.

But when the child does behave, parents tend to miss the opportunity to stroke their kid because they are anticipating the next negative action. The result: Positive behavior from the child is not reinforced, so the child won't repeat those good actions very often. Behavior— both positive and negative—mostly occurs when it is reinforced. Without that reinforcement, it extinguishes itself.

It's also important to notice positive behavior because it gives your defiant child something that everyone enjoys: attention. When kids appear to want only negative attention, it is very likely an illusion. They may simply believe that the only attention they can attract is negative, and they would rather have negative attention than no attention at all.

The Power of Positive Attention

We've dealt with many parents and teachers who understand how powerful positive attention can be and claim that they're already offering it. "I give him plenty of attention," they say, or, "I use praise with him, but it never works." But positive attention is different from just noticing a child and praising him.

Think of all the supervisors or bosses you've ever had. The worst of the lot probably were condescending, critical, micromanaging, nonsupportive, and they probably stole credit for your ideas. The cream of the crop, on the other hand, probably showed appreciation for your hard work, recognized your accomplishments, were supportive, gave you plenty of responsibility, allowed you to make occasional mistakes, were playful, and offered constructive criticism. This second group of bosses used positive attention to motivate you. And more than likely, it worked.

Attention is such a powerful motivator that many people will jump through hoops, solve problems, and work incessantly—all for that subtle, yet oh-so-potent reward of being noticed. On the flip side, people will not work for your attention if they do not respect you and don't find your attention valuable.

Consider one of Bill's patients, a 12-year-old who misbehaved both in school and at home. He lived with his mother and stepfather, who constantly punished and scolded him for bad behavior. The stepfather had an especially sour relationship with the youngster, whom we'll call Terry. Bill told the stepfather that he desperately needed to beef up that relationship if he wanted better compliance from Terry.

This stepfather was a painter, so Bill asked him to think about the jobs he'd done and consider which types of customers he liked the best. The stepfather said he especially liked homeowners who gave him free rein to work as he saw fit and who, after the job was done, showered him with attention and praise. Those jobs, the stepfather said, were great.

Bill then asked about whether he had worked with any not-so-pleasant homeowners. The stepfather quickly remembered one lady who always looked over his shoulder, criticized his work, and second-guessed him. He said that he couldn't wait to finish that job, and that the end product was less than stellar.

Bill interrupted that memory and asked him which type of "home-owner" he was being with his stepson. A light flickered in his eyes, then he hung his head and said, "Oh, now I see."

It didn't take him long, though, to foresee a potential problem with focusing only on the positives. "What do I do about all the times when Terry misbehaves?" asked the stepfather. "Won't he start acting up more if he doesn't get in trouble for it?"

Bill suggested a solution: Because the mother in this family had a strong relationship with Terry, Bill recommended that the stepfather back off the discipline and let Mom handle it. He should just act like a kindly uncle and have fun with his stepson for the next 4 weeks. If the child misbehaved, the stepfather was to mention the problem to his wife and allow her to take whichever action she considered fit.

After 4 weeks, the stepfather reported back that he and his stepson were much closer and that Terry's opposition and defiance had decreased significantly. All problems did not disappear, but they were much more manageable after the stepfather spent 4 weeks being attentive in a positive way.

Misbehavior May Signal a Damaged Relationship

Frequently, we find that a child's opposition and defiance results from a damaged relationship with a parent or teacher. One such case involved Jeremy, a disobedient 9-year-old. His mother was a doctor, and the father was a highly successful consultant who traveled regularly. Mom explained that she had actually witnessed improvements in Jeremy's behavior when Dad was out of town. However, Jeremy's misbehavior not only intensified but was "flat awful" when Dad came home.

Bill asked her to describe a typical day of getting Jeremy ready to go in the morning when Dad was home. While she explained Jeremy's defiance in the morning, the young boy began to chuckle, then laugh harder and harder. Bill asked the mother what Jeremy was laughing about, and she replied: "His dad travels all the time. When he finally does come home, he tries to cram in a whole week's worth of parenting. He micromanages Jeremy. He's critical, so all the two of them do is fight. Jeremy loves getting his father's goat."

Until that point, Bill had assumed that the father had a strong relationship with Jeremy because they were bound by blood and had lived together for the last 9 years. Bill had figured that the pair used whatever brief time they could find together playing games and having fun. It seemed logical that they would have a stable relationship based on trust. Now, Bill realized that he had been wrong. He immediately dropped the therapy that he had planned to suggest and asked the mother to have her husband come in for a visit the next time he was in town.

The father attended the next session and talked in detail about his relationship with both his son and his own father. Not surprisingly, this father had never gotten along with his own dad.

Using a technique that he had learned from his old mentor, Milton Erickson, M.D., Bill asked the father to concentrate on changing the way that he interacted with his son in one area: homework. Then he asked the father to focus only on Jeremy's correct homework problems and not attempt to fix the mistakes.

Jeremy's father worked hard at only noticing the correct examples on his son's homework for 3 weeks. When the father reported back, he said that while it was difficult to break his habit of being critical, the response from Jeremy was overwhelmingly positive. Lately, whenever Dad was in town, the boy would pull out his homework and want his father to see it. The satisfaction in Dad's voice was evident when he said that it was the first time Jeremy had been excited that his dad was home rather than out of town.

We advise starting out with positives because your relationship with your defiant child may well be damaged. As a way to repair that broken bond, you need to smooth it over and work on it using more positive attention.

Be careful, though. You don't want to suffocate the child with praise, because that causes a whole new bag of problems. We adults gain respect in a child's eyes by retaining control and not going into rages or having temper tantrums ourselves. But we also keep that respect by being honest with the child.

Why You Should Spend Time with Your Child

While writing this book, our hearts were tugged every couple of months when the somber news of another school shooting came over the radio, television, or newspaper. Each time, the images on the TV screen were undeniably familiar: Blood-bathed students fleeing school with tears streaming down their faces . . . a handcuffed schoolmate being escorted to the local courthouse . . . local residents talking about how stunned they were that this tragedy happened in their quiet little rural or sub-urban town . . . shocked family and friends of the accused asking, "Why would this child do this?"

We'd like to say that we have all the answers. Unfortunately, we don't. It has taken years for this problem to grow as large as it has. Nothing is going to make it disappear overnight. In fact, we fear that the shootings that took place during the writing of this book are not the end, but the beginning.

Why? Because of a shift in many kids' behavior. When teachers and counselors were asked about the suspects in each shooting, the replies were similar: "Kids these days are angrier than children were in the past." They often added that the children were angry because the important adults in their lives weren't supervising them enough.

While we don't have any instant cures for antisocial behavior, we want to offer you the best advice we can for ensuring that your child won't be involved in a tragedy like the ones we've been discussing. Our advice: Make more time for your child.

We're not talking about spending time during a structured activity like an athletic event where there's no chance to talk. We just want you to "hang out" with your child. You may have heard about the impor-tance of *quality* time, but we're not talking about that. We're talking about spending some *quantity* time with your child.

Ray's wife, Susan, has this concept down. She has taught Ray dozens of lessons about raising children. Almost daily, Susan and their young daughter Rachel engage in some fun and spontaneous activity like painting or watching a movie for the umpteenth time.

A former compulsive worker, Ray used to squeeze in every oppor-tunity to work or be productive throughout the day. When he'd take Rachel to the park, he'd be on a car phone or he'd listen to the news on the radio. At the park, he'd read a book or the paper. Very rarely did he just hang out and relax with his daughter.

Why would a child psychologist behave like this? Because when he did relax, he had programmed himself to feel guilty about not "providing" for his family. What he had been missing was that he hadn't been providing what his daughter needed most.

These days, Ray drives with the radio and phone off. When he takes Rachel to the park, he sits down and watches her play and pushes her on the swing. Ray has gotten more involved in activities like walking his daughter to school or giving her a bath, and once a week he leaves work early to pick Rachel up from school and "hang out."

It's not always easy. Many times, Ray could justify staying at work. But in his practice, Ray has seen the results of children left unattended or shortchanged of quantity time with their parents. He doesn't want Rachel to end up that way.

How Hanging Out Helps a Defiant Child

Spending quantity time is especially important with a defiant child because it shows that there is more to your relationship than just angry words. Even just "neutral" time together will help.

Bill and his stepson, Nick, had an awkward relationship when Bill first married Nick's mother. Bill and Nick both play music, so Bill would allow Nick to use his musical equipment. But trouble began to pop up because Nick would neglect to turn the electronic equipment off, or he would carelessly leave a guitar on the floor where it could be easily trampled. When confronted, Nick would either deny the deed or claim that it was no big deal.

After some time and several conflicts, Bill and Nick's relationship consisted of either avoiding one another or brief, tense confrontations, with Bill threatening to withdraw Nick's privilege of using the equipment.

One day, Bill was on his way to visit a local musical equipment store. As he was about to head out the door, he asked Nick whether he'd like to ride along to look at the instruments. Nick decided to go. They spent an hour or so in the music store, sometimes showing each other instruments and sometimes wandering off on their own. On the way home, Bill asked Nick if he wanted to stop off for a burger, and Nick agreed.

They didn't discuss anything heavy during the lunch or the trip home. Nick thanked Bill for including him on the outing. For the next week or two, Bill noticed that the two of them got along a lot better than usual. The musical equipment was left in better shape when Nick was finished with it. Bill wasn't so uptight about finding something out of place. Several times, Nick even thanked Bill for letting him use the equipment.

It seemed that merely spending a small amount of neutral, conflict-free time together had deposited some credit into Bill and Nick's relationship bank. They weren't bouncing so many checks with one another when little problems happened.

Listening to Your Child

Another way that you gain respect from your child is by spending time listening to him. Kids love to be heard. Ray's wife realized this a long time ago, and she constantly amazes him with how she relates to their daughter. The two of them will sit down and color and have discussions on topics that Ray considers totally inane. But to a child, they are very important subjects. Ray's wife knows how to respond appro-

BEHAVIOR BASICS

Three Ways to Reduce Defiance

1. *Focus on the positives.* Defiant children usually hear nothing but criticism. Acknowledging their good behavior encourages them to repeat the good acts.
2. *Spend* quantity *time with your child.* Neutral, conflict-free time—and lots of it—helps your child see you beyond the role of disciplinarian. This strengthens your relationship.
3. *Set aside some "listening time."* Children will tell you what's on their minds when they feel that it's safe to talk. You need to be there when they're ready.

priately, and she reacts to each sentence as though it were filled with great importance. This is currency that you can deposit in the relationship bank.

Just as important, when kids know that you are available to them, they are more likely to approach you and talk about what's on their minds. They'll usually choose opportunities when you least expect it, such as while you're making dinner or sweeping out the garage.

Children talk when it is safe for them, not when it's convenient for parents. So before you spend your entire weekend working at the office or doing household chores, we hope that you'll stop and take stock. How important will that promotion, clean laundry, or a beautiful garden be if you blow the biggest job of your life: raising your child?

When you listen to, spend neutral time with, or pay attention to your child, you'll find that your relationship will improve. The positives show your child that there's something good in his relationship with you—something to look forward to. They build the relationship so that when you must use negatives, they are within a context of connection and caring, not just punitive measures designed to control and reform the youngster.

11

When Praise Doesn't Work

. . . Here's Something
That Does

Over the years, many teachers have told us that they've tried to change the behavior of defiant children by praising them, "but it just does not work." They'll recall how they praised a child and then saw that same child turn around and put gum in someone's hair or misbehave in some other way.

The teachers are right, of course. Praise doesn't work. That's because a defiant child doesn't need praise to boost his pride. Instead, he needs *acknowledgments*—statements that help him figure out who he is.

Acknowledgments are a way of showing appreciation without having your remarks backfire on you. They're a powerful way to alter your child's behavior. The reason that acknowledgments work better than praise is because they fit with a defiant child's self-image.

Each of us has a self-image, or concept of what we are, who we are, and how we appear to other people. We have an image that we are either short, tall, or medium; fat, thin, or average; and good, bad, or average students. If someone says something that does not match our self-image, we undergo a great deal of stress.

If someone walked up to Ray, for example, and said, "Dr. Levy, you're a great cook," Ray would be stressed because he knows he's a lousy cook. But if that same person had said, "Ray, you're a crummy chef but a very funny guy," he would not feel stressed, because he uses humor as an icebreaker in conversations.

The same principle works with defiant children. Let's say that you are a teacher, and every day you have to get on one of your students, Bobby, for acting up in class. He has a self-image that he is a bad student, disruptive, and something of a class clown. Bobby's self-esteem, on the other hand, might be quite good. He might relish the thought of being the class clown.

If you suddenly said, "Bobby, you are behaving so well. I really like how you're being attentive today. You are such a good student," that assessment would collide with Bobby's self-image. It would disturb him deeply because he does not see himself as a good student. He would probably get upset, and the only way he would know to handle the situation would be to misbehave.

Before you knew it, you'd be back at his desk, saying, "Bobby, what is the problem with you? You were doing so well just a minute ago. What's wrong with you now?"

And as soon as Bobby heard your negative comment, he would feel relief because you would be reassuring him that his self-image was right. Your statement would match the way he sees himself.

This is why we recommend that adults use acknowledgments rather than praise with defiant kids. With an acknowledgment, you simply comment objectively on the youngster's behavior. It's the same thing that Joe Friday used to ask for in the TV show *Dragnet*: "The facts, Ma'am, just the facts."

Here's an example: Let's say that you see Bobby working on

schoolwork rather than pouring glue in his neighbor's hair. You could acknowledge this by saying, "Hey, I noticed that you're writing." You would not need to elaborate on how much you like the behavior. You wouldn't even want to let Bobby know that his actions are good and proper. The goal is to just stick with the facts and avoid value judgments.

As you begin to acknowledge more, two things will start to happen. First, the defiant child will begin listening to you more because your comments are positive or at least non-negative, so it's more fun to listen to you. And second, the acknowledgments will begin to shape the kid's behavior.

Remember, praise contains value judgments, but acknowledgments are simply a statement of fact.

Getting into the Habit of Acknowledging

When parents tell us that their children never do anything to deserve positive acknowledgments, we know that they're simply not used to making these kinds of statements to their children.

One way to get into the habit is to use what we call the hit-and-run technique. To accomplish this, take 10 Post-it notes, draw smiley faces on them, and place them in various places throughout your house: on the refrigerator, in your medicine cabinet, or on top of one of your shoes. When you come across one of these Post-its in the course of the day, find your child and make a statement to him.

You don't have to catch your child doing good things; you just have to catch him *not misbehaving*. For example: "Hey, I noticed that you are watching television with your little sister."

At that point, you need to leave the room as soon as possible. Why leave? Because we parents tend to hold grudges and we'll likely spoil a perfectly good acknowledgment by extending it with a negative comment like "So why couldn't you have done this yesterday? There was really no reason to pick on her then, was there?"

Plop.

If you fall into this routine, all the air will fizzle out of your acknowledgment. That's why we recommend the hit-and-run.

Of course, if your child is misbehaving when you find the Post-it, you don't acknowledge. If he is fighting with his little brother, you wouldn't say, "I noticed that you landed a left hook on your brother's jaw." Clearly, you need to break up the fight or do whatever is necessary to restore order.

For teachers, we recommend placing 10 paper clips in your left pocket each morning. Your goal is to make 10 acknowledgments to your defiant student throughout the morning. Each time you acknowledge, transfer one paper clip from your left pocket to your right. Repeat this procedure in the afternoon. This helps you monitor yourself and get into a new habit. Remember: Without practice, we all tend to fall back into old habits.

BEHAVIOR BASICS

Acknowledgments vs. Praise

▶ **PRAISE**

> **Explanation:** A comment on the child's desired/appropriate behavior that also includes a value judgment or feeling from the commentator
>
> **Examples:** "Oh what a pretty picture." "You're such a good boy."

▶ **ACKNOWLEDGMENT**

> **Explanation:** A description of the child's desired/appropriate behavior. Must be specific and without value or feeling statements. Give as a hit-and-run (say quickly and exit the scene or be quiet).
>
> **Examples:** "I notice that you two boys are sitting quietly in the backseat." "You're eating with your spoon."

The 10-to-1 Ratio

Acknowledgments are the capital that you invest to change your child's behavior. If you want him to listen when you have to make negative comments or redirect his behavior, you need to vastly overcompensate with appreciation and acknowledgments when he is doing what you want him to.

In fact, a good rule is to hand out at least 10 acknowledgments for every single negative comment. A negative comment might be: "You didn't make your bed." Every time you use a downer like that, you need to balance the scales by throwing 10 positives at the youngster during the day. Otherwise, your child will start tuning you out again. Then he won't realize that you also notice the good things that he does.

Rewarding Small Changes

Even the Little Things
Can Mean a Lot

In the past few pages, we've touched on a number of ways that parents and teachers can give their children positive attention. Remember that defiant children need to know when their behavior is appropriate just as badly as they need to know when they are misbehaving. And they need to hear you acknowledge their behavior changes even if they are small.

As adults, we commonly make the mistake of not noticing the little things that our kids do to get headed in the right direction. Instead, we tend to wait until we see a huge change before commenting. With an attitude like that, we're in for a long wait. The fact is, big changes will never arrive if we ignore the small ones.

If you want your child to get headed in the right direction, pay close attention to the specific, concrete evidence that his behavior is improving—no matter how tiny the improvements may seem. By doing so, you will help him transition into better behavior and develop better relationships with others.

One way to get into the habit of recognizing your child's improvements is a technique that we call rewarding small changes. It is amazingly powerful but often underutilized.

Take the case of a ninth grader that Ray counseled. A bright boy, this young man was angry at his overly critical father and was flunking in school to spite him. When Ray asked the father what the first sign of improvement would be, the father responded, "When my son is making all A's."

"Hold it," responded Ray. "Wouldn't that be the last sign?"

"No," the father retorted. "He's a very smart boy. He could make A's and B's with just a little studying."

Ray attempted to educate this father about how *not* noticing movement in the right direction could discourage his son. Unfortunately, the father was unrelenting. His son ultimately failed the ninth grade.

Children have to be allowed to savor their small victories. When they revel in their small accomplishments, they will persevere and turn their little feats into big accomplishments.

How can you reward your child's changes? By following this seven-step program.

1. Target a specific behavior that you'd like to change. Examples might be not getting dressed on time in the morning, or hitting a younger sibling.

2. Picture the behavior that you want to see instead and describe it to yourself in a "video example." This means creating a concrete illustration that a child would be able to see on a videotape, rather than a vague description. For instance, if you can picture a child getting dressed, 10 people watching a video of it would have to agree that the child is getting dressed.

   Use very specific language in developing your video example. Don't just say "Behave!" or "Improve your attitude." Neither of these commands provides enough detail to explain exactly what you want. Also, make sure that your video example pictures an active, positive step that you want your child to take. Don't just describe something like "not hitting anymore"—not hitting is what he *won't* be doing! Think of what you'd like your child to do instead of his misbehavior—perhaps walking into the other room when he gets angry with his sibling, or getting dressed for school on time.

3. Write down the answer to this question: "What will be the very first sign that my child is changing?" When you are figuring out the first sign of change, make it the smallest possible observable behavior that you'll see. Don't go overboard and expect too much. Playing quietly with his brother for 2 minutes or putting on one piece of clothing in the morning are small examples of progress. Therefore, if the child gets one sock on, that is the very first sign that things are headed in the right direction.

4. Tell your child what you're after. Sit down and directly explain to your child what the problem behavior is, which behavior you would rather see instead, and what the first sign of change might be. Give your child a chance to say what he feels the first sign of change might be. If your child suggests something different from what you were hoping to hear, evaluate his thoughts. If his idea is not moving in a negative direction, you ought to seriously consider accepting it.

5. Watch for a time when your child is not engaging in another misbehavior and when he is taking the first step toward the targeted positive behavior.

   Acknowledge the first time you notice a change. If your child is putting that first article of clothing on without being told to, tell him: "I noticed that you're putting on your shirt without being told!"

6. Remind your child that you've noticed his progress. Leave small notes in the child's room, lunchbox, or desk two to three times a day acknowledging his success. For example, if your child did his homework before watching television the night before, you could write a brief note acknowledging this and put it in his lunchbox. These notes are necessary because kids

accustom themselves to blocking out your negative comments, so they naturally begin blocking your positive ones as well.

7. Monitor your child's positive change in a journal. This helps you keep track of progress and stay encouraged.

When using this method, it's important to break down the target behavior into small enough pieces that you'll have many opportunities to acknowledge improvement. Also make sure to note each time that there is change.

Two Mistakes That Can Stifle Success

We adults are capable of making two mistakes when using this seven-step program, and they both can cause the child to stop improving: One is not noticing slight improvements, and the other is giving back-handed compliments.

Sometimes it can be hard to find improvement in the behavior of a defiant child. But you must search for positives, however slight, if you want to promote change. Take the case of a young boy named Dennis. He used to hit his mother whenever he got frustrated. Dennis's mother not only wound up with massive bruises but also had hurt feelings and a damaged relationship with her only child.

Finally, after some time, Dennis stopped hitting his mother and started cussing her out instead. We're not condoning the verbal behavior, but it did mark an end to the physical—and more serious—abuse. Thus, it was worth noting.

During a quiet time, the mother mentioned to him that she was aware that he wasn't hitting her anymore and that he was using his words instead. Later, during another quiet time, she told him that she would like him to use different words when expressing his anger.

Initially, this mother struggled to see how cursing was a step up from hitting. She was tempted to punish him for cursing, and she nearly missed an opportunity to acknowledge the shift in his behavior. Of course, the mother did not condone the cursing. In fact, eventually, the child did get in trouble for cursing. But acknowledging initially that cursing was a slight movement in the right direction helped her

BEHAVIOR BASICS

Seven Steps That Change Behavior

1. Target a specific behavior that you'd like to change.
2. Describe to yourself the behavior that you want to see in a "video example."
3. Write down the answer to this question: "What will be the very first sign that my child is changing?"
4. Tell your child what you're after.
5. When your child is involved in that targeted positive behavior, acknowledge that you are noticing it.
6. Leave small notes reminding your child that you're noticing his progress.
7. Track your child's positive change in a journal.

strengthen her relationship with the child so that he was more inclined to listen to her.

The other pitfall to watch out for is dishing out the backhanded compliment: "Hey, you got your socks and pants on! Now, if you had done this yesterday, we wouldn't have had the same struggle, would we?" Don't do this, tempting though it may be.

We must all realize that children don't jump from misbehaving to behaving properly all in one day. Instead, they do it one step at a time. A child may move from a full-scale tantrum of lying on the floor kicking and screaming to a temper tantrum where he just yells and stomps in his room. Eventually, he will learn to change this behavior and instead talk with you about his frustrations. Remember that change occurs gradually.

Our message? Watch for subtle changes.

Chapter 13

The Power of Playtime

Four Ways That Playing Can Improve Your Relationship with Your Child

*I*f you have a young child—say, under the age of 8 or 9—and you are reading this book, chances are awfully good that you often complain that your child doesn't listen to you. In fact, that solitary problem—children not listening—is the catalyst for most of the anguish suffered in American homes today.

We have a solution. Play with your child.

Yes, it sounds too simple. But if you do it right, playing with your child can teach him to listen instead of tuning you out, and it can improve your overall relationship. In this chapter, we'll explain four ways to put child's play to serious work. Interested? Read on.

Attending to Play

Here's a scary fact: Between 80 and 90 percent of the average parent's conversation with a child is not very rewarding for the child. You may find that hard to believe, but think about it: Comments like "Johnny, get your pajamas on!" aren't punishing, but they aren't pleasing either.

When your defiant child hears comment after comment like that, he's likely to learn to tune you out—if he isn't tuning you out already. We have a solution. It's a technique called Attending to Play that was developed by Russell Barkley, Ph.D., a psychologist and researcher at the University of Massachusetts Medical School who has authored many books and articles on attention deficit hyperactivity disorder.

Attending to Play is designed to increase your child's compliance and positive behaviors by improving his ability to listen to you. It provides opportunities for you to comment positively on your child's actions. That will help you slowly open him back up and coax him into listening to you again. Not only will it enhance your youngster's listening skills but it will also simultaneously improve his relationship with you.

Before we explain Attending to Play, we must warn you of a few pitfalls:

1. This technique doesn't work very well with children older than 8.
2. It requires a good deal of time. (Though it is time-consuming, getting your child to listen better may well be worth the investment.)
3. It is not terribly exciting for the parent, so it takes a good deal of perseverance to succeed with it.

Also, note that there are some rules about when and how to use this technique. (See "The Key Rules of Attending to Play" on page 104 for cautions.)

Okay, there's the "manufacturer's warning." Now here's how Attending to Play works.

The next time you see your defiant child playing, sit down on the same level as him. If he's at the table, pull up a chair. If he's out in the sandbox, don't be afraid to get your clothes dirty. (It will be worth the dry-cleaning bill.) And if he's on the floor, get right down there with him.

The next step is to narrate as your child plays. Now, you're prob-

The Key Rules of Attending to Play

1. Do not ask questions. Questions tend to distract children. For instance, imagine that your child is playing with some building blocks. If you point at a toy car to his right and ask, "Isn't that your favorite car, Roy?", that will disrupt the attention he was giving to his blocks. Attending to Play should be totally child-driven: Where he sits, you sit; when he plays, you narrate.

2. Do not criticize or punish, if at all possible. If the child starts misbehaving, it is your duty to ignore it and walk away. However, children rarely misbehave when they are playing and being attended to in a positive fashion.

3. Don't try to stage the activity. The child must be playing at an activity of his choice—not doing schoolwork or a chore. It must be the kid's decision, not yours.

4. Do not attempt this if your child is watching television or playing a computer game. That would drive us crazy, and we suspect that it would drive you crazy as well.

ably asking what exactly we're talking about when we say *narrate*. The answer is simple: Become a play-by-play radio announcer for your child. A good example of a radio announcer is Gene Peterson, who has called Houston Rockets basketball games on the air for years. Here's a sampling of his play-by-play announcing: "Hakeem Olajuwon turns and spins to the bucket. . . . Holy cow, Hakeem somehow put the ball in!! *How sweet it is!*"

It's your turn now. If you find your child building a wall with Lego blocks and then taking his toy car and crashing into it, get down on his level and say something like "And he's putting the gray Legos on top of the green platform. My goodness, he's building a skyscraper. It's getting way up there. And now—look at this—he's taking a car *[big-time enthusiasm in your voice]*! It's barreling down the runway and—Whack! Smack! Bam!—*It slams into the wall!*"

When your child kicks a ball around the backyard, you can casually narrate while barbecuing or just relaxing on the porch: "He kicks the ball into the corner, and now he's fighting to get it out. One, two, three kicks, and he's dribbling along the fence line!"

If your child wants to ride his bike down the street, all you need to do is sit on the front steps. When he finishes and pulls up on the driveway or sidewalk, you can comment: "Boy, you sure were pedaling hard." There's no need to get a bullhorn and narrate so all the neighbors can hear you. Just one comment does the trick.

Remember, it is really the attention you give your child that has a profoundly positive effect. Once your child realizes that your attention is generally positive, he won't turn you off as much. The purpose of this exercise is to train your child to tune you in.

This is simply pure, unadulterated attention. In more than 50 combined years of clinical practice, we have yet to find a child who does not enjoy this. We have heard of children who do not like their parents narrating and prefer that their parents just watch, but all children soak up the attention.

Another way to approach this exercise is to imagine that a blind person is with you and that you are telling him exactly what your child is doing. When reporting, you are not using your opinion. You are just narrating.

Perform this one-on-one with your child, not with other children around. If you're a single parent with several children, bag this idea. It will require too much of your time and resources. Instead, in that case, you should step up use of the acknowledgments and other exercises in this book. Attending to Play will help, but it is not mandatory.

Training Yourself to Attend to Play
The top problem most parents have when Attending to Play is that they start asking questions rather than just commenting. This is natural enough. As a parent, you are accustomed to asking questions for several reasons.

First, when your child was a toddler, you probably led him to specific answers by asking him questions such as "How many ears does the doggie have?" This naturally got you into a pattern.

Second, when your child was young, you likely asked questions as a way of testing his knowledge on a subject. You wanted to know if he was attaining the correct developmental milestones or was lagging behind in a certain area.

However, when you are Attending to Play, questions can distract— or even stress out—your child. In order to break this habit, it helps to practice with another adult. Ask your spouse or someone else to sit and listen to you narrate, and to remind you with hand signals when you begin to ask a question. Practice also helps because you must do this exercise often with your child for it to be effective.

For this technique to work, we recommend that you attend to play for 15 to 20 minutes, three or four times a week. You can break up this time into 10 minutes here and 10 minutes there, but we recommend that you not attend to play for less than 10 minutes in a single setting.

The point of this exercise is not to prepare you for a career in broadcasting professional sporting contests. No, the focus is much more important than that: You are giving your child pure attention in exchange for his good behavior. The child is clearly behaving while playing whichever game he wants. Meanwhile, you are getting your kiddo into the rhythm of listening to you.

We have received mostly positive feedback from parents who have implemented this procedure. Most parents report that children are significantly calmer and more attentive after just a week of Attending to Play.

Why Free-Form Play Is So Important

Are you busy?

Do you wake up in the morning with a million things to do? Do you go to bed each night with 999,999 things left undone? Do you rush to get the biscuits out of the oven for breakfast, rush to get the kids to school, rush to get yourself to work on time, rush through the grocery store in order to pick up the kids from soccer on time?

You are not alone. That's how our society is designed these days. Keep up or get off the bus. You'll lose your job to some young thoroughbred right out of college if you don't stay late at work two or three times a week.

As we enter a new century, we often have difficulty relaxing— taking time out for leisure. We often run our errands on the weekends, and Sundays (or Saturdays) are rarely the days of relaxation that God intended them to be.

Not only do we push ourselves to the max; we also push our children to the max. Play between parents and children is much more structured and stressful today than it was 20 or 40 years ago. But play is every bit as important to the moral, ethical, cognitive, and emotional development of youngsters as it was 40 years ago.

In his book *The Hurried Child*, David Elkind, Ph.D., notes that play is how children unwind and de-stress from their difficult days at school. The average child spends approximately 7 hours a day in school learning and dealing with the pressures of new academic material and peers. After a day of this, it is extremely important that children have time to play as a method of unwinding.

But playing by itself is not enough. Play needs to be a time of pure recreation for the child, just as we discussed in the last section. The best way to stress a child out more than he already is would be to intervene in his play and to structure it in a way that isn't natural for him. This most often happens in organized sports.

Recently, Ray took his daughter swinging at a park near their home. While she was swinging, a group of kids and their parents set up some traffic cones to mark off a soccer field and goals. One parent/coach helped these 5-year-old boys learn how to dribble the black-and-white checkered ball and pass to one another. The expressions on the youngsters' faces said that they were more interested in playing with each other and the ball on their own terms. They had no clue what they were supposed to do or what was expected of them.

The boys probably didn't find that experience relaxing and helpful, but they probably thought that their parents enjoyed it. And they were behaving to please their parents, not themselves.

We believe that kids would enjoy play more if their parents would take them to a park, drop a couple of balls on the field, and let *them* choose which game they want to play, how they want to play, and which rules they want to use while their parents sit a safe distance away—intruding only to keep the peace when major squabbles arise.

Playing with You

This next part may seem to contradict what we just wrote about tossing a ball in the field and letting kids decide which game they want to play. But hear us out: There's a good point just ahead. Here's the "contradiction": Kids need to play not only with each other but also with the adults in their lives, in order to learn the importance of rules.

In all honesty, this does not contradict our earlier statement. You don't want to interfere, but you do want the kids to set rules, even if the rules are their own and not yours.

One way that you can play with your child on his terms is to let him choose the activity and then do it the way that he wants to do it. Go outside and ride bikes with your son, following the course that he sets. Or shoot a few hoops with your daughter in a game that she creates.

And, whatever the activity, just enjoy the chance to play with your child. In our practices, we play with clients during therapy. Most little boys like to be roughhoused, so we occasionally give them "Dutch rubs" or "noogies" (head rubs with the knuckles). Ray also has a whoopee cushion in his office, which most pre-adolescent boys find absolutely hilarious.

Verbally Playing

The way that we as therapists play verbally is by not taking everything our patients say to heart. This is a good rule for parents to follow too.

A classic example is the day when Ellen walked into Ray's office. An 11-year-old adoptee, Ellen was in total control of her household. Her parents and siblings walked on eggshells, doing all they could to not stir her anger. Ellen was a beautiful young girl, but she had done all she could to appear ghostly. She had dyed her blond hair white, wore pasty makeup, and dressed only in black clothes. Among other inappropriate activities, she was sexually involved with a 12-year-old boy.

The parents exerted zero control over any of this. During one session, Ray began trying to correct the hierarchy by showing her parents different ways to set and enforce rules. As he spoke to the parents, he focused all his attention on them as though they were in authority, not Ellen. The young girl attempted to break in. Whenever she tried to interrupt, Ray would signal with his hand for her to be quiet while keeping his gaze intent on her parents. Feeling ignored and demoted in the rankings of her household, Ellen grew hopping mad. She butted in a few times, huffed often, and rolled her eyes constantly.

Before long, she realized that some rules these adults were discussing would seriously infringe on her independence. She didn't like the prospective amendments to household policy. From the corner of Ray's eye, he could see a storm brewing. Ellen was holding the couch so tightly that her arms started shaking. She was on the verge of screaming.

When the adults finally reached a point where she could take no more, she exploded: "You're a butthead!" The defaming remark was made in Ray's general direction because, after all, things had been just fine in her world until this counselor person got in the way.

The room grew quiet, and her parents' eyes grew bigger and looked at Ray as if to say, "All right, Mr. Hotshot Therapist. What are you going to do now?" Ray quietly switched his gaze to focus on Ellen for the first time since the session began. He flashed a stern look at her and said, "Young lady, I treat you with respect. I expect you to treat me with respect, too. I have never name-called or spoken disparagingly toward you in here, and I expect the same courtesy from you. I find what you just said offensive. I worked many years to earn my title. From now on when you address me, I expect you to call me 'Dr. Butthead'!"

The tension immediately dissipated from the room. From that moment on, Ellen called Ray "Dr. Butthead," which was fine with him. The lesson is that Ray did not take everything she said seriously; instead, he added some play to it. The results? Ray's relationship with her improved, as did her parents' relationship with her—once they began to lighten up as well.

BEHAVIOR BASICS

Putting Playtime to Work

1. *Narrate your child's activities.* This gets him accustomed to hearing you say positive things about him, and it encourages him to listen.

2. *Provide time for free-form play.* Kids need unstructured R&R just as adults do. Organized sports don't count.

3. *Play by his rules.* Play with your child, but let him pick the game and the rules.

4. *Verbally play with your child.* Don't take everything he says seriously.

Play is an essential component in life—one that we often miss out on. Along with acknowledgments, rewarding small changes, and Attending to Play, play itself is a key way to improve your relationship with the child in your life.

Tracking Progress

Often, parents can grow discouraged about how long it takes to see improvement in their child's behavior. A good way to deal with this is to chart your child's progress in a notebook. Writing down the dates and times of every improvement you notice will keep you from losing sight of how far your child has come.

This concept of charting is not much different from the way your parents kept track of your height when you were growing up. You had no way to watch yourself grow, so marking where the top of your head reached on a wall once a month allowed you to see that you were actually progressing. Charting will also keep you in a positive frame of mind and decrease the negativity with which you otherwise might view your defiant child.

5

Part

You Solve It, or I'll Solve It . . . and You Won't Like My Solution

Defiant kids seem to need more intense positives and negatives than average kids before they get motivated to change. In this part, we detail a number of methods for finally winning back control from your child when he has had the upper hand.

What you want is for your child to start solving the problem that he has caused for others. The basic philosophy here is: "You solve the problem, or I'll solve it for you . . . and you won't like my solution." Once the child gets a taste of your solution, he will become more motivated and more active in solving the problem before you do, because he hates to lose control in the way that these methods will require him to.

Whether your child is into control or is just entirely inflexible, this section will help you regain control and start to build flexibility in him.

14

Training Camp

How to Put Yourself Back in Charge
(Be like a Boy Scout: Be Prepared)

Very few situations in American life are as trying on the spirit and soul as boot camps held by the United States military. If you have ever spoken with people who attended a boot camp—whether in the army, air force, navy, or marines—they probably mentioned that the experience pushed them to their breaking point at least once.

The primary purpose of military boot camps is to discipline and mold the independent streaks of young soldiers. Once discipline has been established, the maturing troops obey orders the instant they are given. This obedience is especially vital in life-or-death situations that soldiers encounter in the heat of battle.

Training Camps for kids are much like those boot camps. They are designed to help your child realize that you are in charge and that he is ultimately not in control.

Although you don't want your child to snap a salute every time you walk into the room, it is vital that your child respect you. And though parents will never require their children to fire weapons at the enemy, there are times when instant compliance would be nice.

Unfortunately, earning that respect and obedience is not simple. Just like the military officer who leads his troops through the mud, sleet, and snow on 15-mile hikes, your endurance will be tested. Your test may come when your screaming child reaches that one unbearable screech and you start thinking about giving in. Or the test might come when your child tries to manipulate you into solving problems for him.

When beginning a Training Camp for your child, the most important thing to keep clear is that you are the commanding officer. You must not allow your child to take charge when he is being disciplined. You call the shots. Beyond that rule, you need to follow these three steps to finally break your child's pattern of defiance and control of the situation:

1. Pick one misbehavior.
2. Pick a time.
3. Do something different.

Step 1: Pick One Misbehavior

Parents are often confronted with so many misbehaviors that they try to correct the child for everything inappropriate that he does, and they wind up not even making a dent. You must recognize that your defiant child has more energy than you and that you will be more effective if you choose one problem to focus on at a time.

One way to do this is to make a list and select one behavior that is most agitating to you. Be specific. Don't list things like "bad attitude" or "noncompliant"; these are too vague. Pick a "video example"— something that if recorded on videotape would be clear to anyone who watched it. Examples might be "doesn't clean up dinner plate" or "picks on sister in minivan."

The more specific you are, the easier it will be to track the progress and to come up with a plan.

Ray had a client who told him, "Mornings are impossible." If she could just make mornings more peaceful, she believed, the rest of her day would go much more smoothly, even though more problems might pop up when she returned home each afternoon.

Ray asked her to be more specific because "mornings" was too vague to focus on. After questioning her, Ray discovered that getting her children up and getting dressed were not the problems. The true difficulties were that her two daughters bickered at the breakfast table and didn't pack their book bags. Mom decided to focus on breakfast table quarreling as the target misbehavior. With a clear, specific behavior selected, she could then choose a time and develop a strategy for changing the behavior.

Step 2: Pick a Time

When selecting the best time to focus on your child's behavior, choose a time that is most convenient for you. Otherwise, your defiant child will pick a time that is most convenient for him and least convenient for you. Children rarely misbehave when it's inconvenient for them— like when they want a ride to the mall.

The mother Ray spoke to was most inconvenienced by the morning quarreling. But her children were in no rush to get to school on time (what a surprise). Being late didn't bother them one bit. So it didn't make sense for Mom to tackle the problem and provide a consequence at that time.

She and Ray talked about having the children practice table etiquette after school for half an hour. Mother quickly came up with all the reasons that that would not work. First, one daughter had dance on Mondays and Wednesdays, so the solution would not work on those days. The other daughter had soccer on Thursdays. And Mom was busy on Fridays, so Tuesdays were all that was left.

Ray asked the mother, "What's more important: soccer practice or learning a valuable coping skill that will last a lifetime? Is it worth missing a few dance lessons, or would you rather be held hostage every morning until these girls are 18?"

Next, Mom was concerned that she would lose money by missing the practice sessions. Ray's answer: "Anything that's cheaper than one therapy session is worth it, considering how expensive a therapy session is."

The best time to focus on a misbehavior is a time that's most inconvenient for your child—like during an activity he enjoys, or during a game he'd like to watch on TV, or at a time when he usually plays video games or plays with his friends.

Step 3: Do Something Different

This entire book has been showing ways to come up with different responses to misbehavior. That's the key to getting your child to change.

Time and time again in our therapy practices, we've heard parents say, "Every single day, my child has problems brushing his teeth and getting ready for bed. And every single day, I wind up having to yell at him. When will he ever learn?"

We often find ourselves thinking, "When will you (the parent) ever learn?"

You can expect your child to misbehave; what you need to do is be prepared with a different response when he does. Say to yourself: "I know that my child is going to have trouble getting his teeth brushed. He is telling me that he needs help brushing his teeth and getting ready for bed. Tonight, as he dawdles, I will tell him in a calm voice not to worry; we have plenty of time tomorrow afternoon to practice. Unfortunately, he'll have to practice this rather than going Rollerblading with his friend."

This is being prepared with a different response. Your child is fully expecting you to respond by yelling and screaming; he's already mastered a way to cope with that. But he is not prepared for losing out on Rollerblading time and for having to work on brushing his teeth instead. This will be a drag, and it will very likely motivate him to stop dawdling and get ready for bed on his own.

When you expect and plan for a misbehavior, you won't be caught off guard, and you'll be able to manufacture a new plan. Too many times, parents expect the best and wind up with the worst. Don't get caught by surprise. If you expect the worst and plan for it, you'll wind up with the best.

If your child is prone to using the same old lines such as "It's not fair" or "I don't love you," make up your mind to ignore the cries or use a brain-dead phrase like those we listed in "Brain-Dead Phrases You Can Use" on pages 70–71. Decide before the fact that you will not be affected by what he says—no matter how dramatic your child's response may be.

The best way to prepare is to practice. Ask your spouse or a friend to play the role of your child so that you can have a "dress rehearsal."

Practice takes on an even greater importance if your child constantly comes up with new and increasingly bothersome remarks in an attempt to break up your disciplinary actions. A child like this is simply trying to escalate the tension until you are no longer in control. That way, he will be able to manipulate you the same way he always has. So ahead of time, act out exactly what may happen, and make a commitment that nothing will prevent you from regaining control of your child.

Being prepared might also mean looking to others for support. This gives you that all-important peace-of-mind. For example, it is particularly important that you make neighbors aware of potentially loud temper tantrums your child might throw while you're conducting a Training Camp.

One lady warned all six of her neighbors that she was about to start a Training Camp for Jeffrey, her 9-year-old who had previously refused to go into Time Out. Jeffrey's mother informed neighbors that he might yell and scream for a while each day. She let them know that she would not be abusing the child and that she would use Hold Downs only until he cooperated by going into Time Out. She apologized to the neighbors for Jeffrey's behavior, which had been causing problems in the apartment complex, and she explained that this therapy could curb his inappropriate antics.

All six neighbors were willing to handle the extra noise for a few weeks, and two offered to come and help hold Jeffrey down.

Of course, not all neighbors will be quite so gracious. Nevertheless, it helps just knowing that whenever your son requires physical discipline such as a Hold Down, you won't have to worry about what the neighbors think. And when your child finds out that he can't control you by screaming, he learns that manipulation doesn't work anymore.

Here's another example of how you can prepare: Bill had a child in therapy, Kaitlin, whose parents left her and a younger sister with a babysitter. This girl would give the babysitter a very hard time. She was clearly angry with her parents for leaving and was taking it out on the babysitter. This wasn't fair to the babysitter, and it reinforced bad problem-solving skills in the girl. Often, the babysitter would call the parents on their cell phone, forcing the parents to break up their date and come home to discipline their daughter.

Rather than lecturing Kaitlin about how to behave before they left, the parents needed to come up with a new plan. Bill helped them decide to reserve two babysitters, only one of whom would show up initially. If Kaitlin started misbehaving, the parents would be notified. They would then tell Kaitlin that Miss Jones—her least favorite

BEHAVIOR BASICS

Three Steps to a Successful Training Camp

1. *Pick one behavior that you want to change,* and be specific about what you want your child to do differently.
2. *Pick a time to focus on changing the behavior.* It should be a time when you have the energy to do what needs to be done and to hang in there until you make a breakthrough.
3. *Do something different.* If you respond to your child's misbehavior as you always have, he'll just tune you out or cope with you as he always has. You need to respond in a new way to get his attention and motivate him to change.

babysitter—would be coming over to take care of her alone. Her little sister would get to enjoy the other babysitter. And not only would Kaitlin's bedtime be earlier, but she would also have to figure out how to pay Miss Jones.

The parents had to reserve Miss Jones and pay her whether she came or not, but it was still cheaper than an extra therapy session. In fact, Kaitlin did misbehave, and Miss Jones did have to come over. Kaitlin wound up paying Miss Jones with CDs (even though Miss Jones was really compensated by Kaitlin's father). After that one test, Kaitlin was never a problem for babysitters again.

By following the three steps outlined in this chapter, you will keep your child from catching you off guard with his chronic misbehavior. The good thing about chronic misbehavior, as we've said before, is that you always get a second chance to help change it. In their hearts, defiant children do not like to misbehave. They just need to know who is in control.

The Power of Consequences

Putting the Brakes on Misbehavior
in a Way That Makes Sense

D espite your grand attempts to build a great relationship with your defiant child, there will still be times and situations where he will continue to misbehave or be inflexible.

Your child may still say "Try and make me!" or "You're not the boss of me!" There will still be times when you think that the word *no!* pops from his mouth every other sentence—especially when things aren't going his way. And you may reach the point where you're ready to pull out not only your own hair but your child's hair as well.

That's when you need to call in the troops and make your child responsible for the problems he's causing. How? By giving him consequences that teach him the appropriate way to behave.

Before we move into the specifics of consequences, however, we must remind you how important it is to first ensure that you have a solid relationship with your child. That means practicing the methods we've explained so far, such as acknowledging appropriate behavior, or Attending to Play with young children. Without a good relationship, the techniques we are about to discuss will almost certainly backfire.

Countless times in our experience, teachers and parents have focused too intently on technique and have remained unaware about the significance of the relationship. That causes children to get angrier and angrier, feeling robbed and cheated of their birthright: a connection. When that happens, their behavior intensifies into an inferno rather than improving.

Remember: Without a relationship, everything in this and the next few chapters will only be a series of techniques that turn you into a prison guard in charge of a prisoner. As soon as prison guards turn their backs, prisoners misbehave and scheme against their guards.

Consequences vs. Punishment

Quite often, when adults try to curb a child's defiance, they confuse consequences with punishment. That makes it difficult for them to apply consequences in a way that changes the behavior.

There are two main differences between consequences and punishment. The first is that a consequence teaches your child what you want him to learn, while punishment rarely does.

For instance, imagine for a moment that your child didn't clean up his room as you'd asked him to. As a response, you grounded him from watching television for a few days. That is punishment. Missing television doesn't help him learn how to clean better. It just makes him squirm and wish like hell that he'd cleaned up his room.

Another unwanted side effect of punishment is that your child becomes resentful and acts out in revenge, resulting in another punishment.

On the other hand, a good consequence *educates* your child. It shows him the correct behavior you want in concrete ways he can understand.

In the example of the dirty room, a consequence would be to have your child clean up the room while you watch. Then have him mess up the room again and straighten it again, and have him go through this process two to four more times—with a good attitude. This consequence teaches him what you want him to do: *clean.* It will also make sense to your child, though the task may not necessarily be pleasant.

A second difference between consequences and punishment is the way that each is delivered. Punishment is almost always unleashed during a display of anger. Often, you become angry because your child has hassled or embarrassed you. Your natural response: punishment delivered in a rage, which conveys your emotions. This is a common reaction. We've all done it.

Of course, venting your anger is tempting, and it feels good while you do it. But it just doesn't motivate defiant kids. In fact, it often backfires because defiant children love to get your goat and provoke your ire.

Kids consider this control. When you angrily dish out punishment, you invite your child to struggle with you, not learn a lesson.

On the other hand, if you deliver a consequence with sadness and empathy, you let the child know that the responsibility for the problem rests on *his* shoulders, and no attempt to suck you into the struggle will work. The result: Your child will soon learn to behave, because inappropriate actions only inconvenience *him.*

Now, empathetically issuing a consequence is tough. You naturally feel upset when your kid misbehaves, so it is unnatural for you to respond with sadness and empathy. We understand this and recommend that you *practice* your response first.

If you feel that your anger will prevent you from responding immediately with sadness, then try delaying your response and the consequence. Don't be swayed by parenting books that say that you have to give a consequence as close to the misbehavior as possible. And don't believe their claims that children, especially defiant children and those with attention deficit hyperactivity disorder, won't remember the offense if you delay the consequence.

That line of thinking assumes that these children have difficulty remembering. It is true that they don't remember things that aren't important to them, such as homework. But promise a defiant child that you'll take him to Pizza Hut (or his favorite restaurant) at the end of the week, and see if he forgets.

Delaying the consequence long enough for you to think about it and deliver it more calmly will work like a charm. No harm will be done, and your child will begin learning his lesson.

Of course, we are not suggesting that you delay the consequence deliberately or taunt the child for days promising a consequence. But it's okay to delay telling your child about the consequence for a day, if necessary. Use your own judgment if you think that your child can handle more time or less between the infraction and hearing about the consequence.

One last note: We've explained the differences between punishment and consequences to help you understand why we recommend using consequences first. To your child, consequences will still feel like punishment. But by delivering consequences with empathy or sadness, you make the child angry at the consequence, not you.

Natural vs. Logical Consequences

Consequences usually come in one of two forms: natural or logical. Natural consequences occur as a direct result of the forces of nature. If you do not eat, you get hungry. If you go out in cold weather without a coat on, you get cold. If you don't sleep enough at night, you feel sleepy the next day. These are all natural events. In most cases, you should not interfere if your child does something that will lead to a natural consequence. It is far and away the best teacher.

The only time when you should get in the way of a natural consequence is if it might result in serious or permanent damage—for example, if a child is about to hurt himself by touching a hot stove, running in the street, or patting a dog that is foaming at the mouth and snarling.

But many times, we as adults aren't worried about whether a natural consequence is potentially dangerous. We just don't allow the natural consequence to run its course because, quite frankly, we feel guilty, we just don't want to be bothered dealing with the result, we feel pressured by our timetables, or we want to avoid the fallout of those consequences on ourselves.

We're talking about situations such as when your child wants to walk out into the rain without a raincoat. If you stop your child from heading out the door, it's likely that you're doing it because you don't want to deal with the inconvenience. You don't want to spend the time required—or you simply don't have the time—for him to change into dry clothes afterward. Or you don't want to miss work to care for him if he catches a cold. Or maybe you just feel guilty—that you'll be seen as a bad parent if you let your kid run out in the rain without a vinyl raincoat. In each case, your reaction would prevent your child from learning an important lesson. That's a mistake.

Logical Consequences

Sometimes, natural consequences are not possible. In these cases, logical consequences need to be the teacher.

Logical consequences occur in everyone's life when society works as it should. If you don't pay your heating bill on time, you'll end up shivering in a cold shower. That's a logical consequence. If you rob a store and go to jail, that's your logical consequence. If you run a red light and hit someone's car, you pay for the repairs to both cars, pay for both rental cars while you're both inconvenienced, say "I'm sorry," and then move on—all logical consequences.

Another important characteristic of logical consequences: There usually are no additional penalties. If running that red light was your first offense, the judge wouldn't make you do all the things mentioned above *plus* take away your driving privileges, or ground you at your house over the weekend and take away your telephone privileges.

If there's an opportunity for your child to experience a logical consequence—say, he breaks a neighbor's toy in a rage—then you should let him feel it. Don't pay to replace that toy; let him figure out how to do it. It will help him understand how the world works.

Children should be allowed to feel their own consequences—as long as the consequence is not potentially hazardous—because experiencing a consequence is a vital part of growing up. By robbing a child of these essential experiences, you cheat him out of opportunities to learn and grow. This is especially true for defiant kids, for whom consequences are especially valuable learning experiences.

Constructively Choosing a Consequence

"But Bill and Ray," you might be thinking, "I can't come up with a nifty consequence immediately every time my son misbehaves."

No problem. We'll divide logical consequences into three separate categories—*relevant*, *related*, and *significant*—and we'll help you develop appropriate planned consequences before your child misbehaves.

Your goal in using these types of consequences is to start first with the most effective: relevant ones. Related consequences are next in the flowchart of effectiveness, so they should be your second choice, followed by significant consequences. Because significant consequences most closely resemble punishment, they are the least effective with defiant kids.

Let's look at each type of consequence in detail.

Relevant Consequences

One family that Bill works with has a 12-year-old boy who constantly chewed with his mouth open at the table. His dad constantly nagged him about it, but all the words in the world changed nothing. The boy still smacked loudly while eating, and the father grew more agitated.

One day, it just got to be too much for the father. He threw down his napkin, stood up, and yelled: "Okay. That's it, Jeffrey. You're still chewing with your mouth open. You lose your boom box."

When Jeffrey's father recounted this, Bill was amazed. Boom box in exchange for smacking at the table? Seeing no relation between the two, Bill explained to the father that his response made no sense unless Jeffrey was chewing on the boom box.

Taking the stereo away was designed to hurt the boy, not to discourage him from eating with his mouth open or to teach him how to chew with his mouth closed. What Dad needed to do was provide a relevant consequence—one that helped his son practice the behavior that he wanted the child to change.

Bill suggested that the next time Jeffrey chewed with his mouth open at the table, Dad should calmly say: "Jeff, when you chew like that, it really upsets me and makes dinner a very unpleasant activity. I can tell that you need some practice at chewing with your mouth closed. Instead of shooting hoops with your buddies after school tomorrow, you'll have to practice chewing with your mouth closed for half an hour. Then tomorrow night, I'll notice if you've learned how to do it. If not, you'll be letting me know that you need more practice."

Dad tried the strategy, and after two "practice" days, Jeff found a way to eat with his mouth closed.

This situation got straightened out because the father used a consequence that was relevant to the problem. (A relevant consequence is a consequence that is directly related to the misbehavior and moves your child closer to the desired behavior.)

If you're unclear as to what a relevant consequence would be for your child's most distressing misbehavior, put yourself in a judge's seat. Ask yourself: "What behavior would I rather see instead?" If your child is leaving the table without clearing his plate, then the answer is "Clearing his plate." If your son is throwing a ball inside the house, the answer is "Picking up his ball, walking outside, and *then* throwing it."

Think in terms of what you would rather see instead—not what you'd prefer *not* to see. Most often, that's all you need to do to come up with a good and useful relevant consequence.

Related Consequences

If your adolescent son got caught smoking, the relevant consequence would be for him to breathe clean air. Not a really effective response, is it?

That's when you need to enact a related consequence—one that has a direct relationship to the misbehavior. For example, you could make your adolescent smoker go to the public library, do some research on the dangers of cigarette smoking, and write a five-page paper on the slow and ugly death that would result from continued use of tobacco products. Or if you are the boy's teacher—or have a good relationship with his English instructor—you could have the boy do a lecture on the dangers and hazards of cigarette smoking.

As adults, we receive related consequences all the time. In many parts of the country, when you get pulled over for speeding, you are required to attend a defensive driving course in order to avoid paying for the ticket and having it on your record. Sitting through what is usually a boring diatribe about the dangers of speeding and breaking traffic laws or watching scary movies about terrible accidents is a related consequence. It is directly associated with the misbehavior, though it doesn't necessarily teach you how to drive more safely. If you had to drive with a monitor that wouldn't allow you to speed for a week or a signal that would turn off the stereo in the car every time you went over the speed limit, that would be more of a relevant consequence.

Using the example above about Jeffrey, who was chewing with his mouth open, here's how a related consequence would have remedied the situation. The next time Jeffrey chewed with his mouth open at the table, his dad could say: "Jeff, when you chew like that, it really upsets me and makes dinner a very unpleasant activity. Please do that all you want to in the laundry room. I hope you don't mind picking up your plate and going there so that I can eat peacefully."

After several meals alone in the laundry room, the boy would probably become more motivated to stop annoying his father by beginning to eat with his mouth closed.

Do you see the difference? In the earlier consequence, Jeff had to directly practice the desired behavior (chewing with his mouth closed) at a time that was inconvenient for him (that's why we say, "You solve it, or I'll solve it . . . and you won't like my solution"). That's a relevant consequence. In this case, Jeff didn't have to practice the desired behavior, but the consequence did have something to do with eating with his mouth open. That's a related consequence.

When possible, use these two kinds of consequences to help your child learn appropriate behavior. When it's not possible to use them, you can shift to significant consequences.

Significant Consequences

Way too often, we parents jump immediately to significant consequences without allowing natural consequences to take their course and before attempting relevant or related consequences.

Significant consequences are usually "hurtful" or "attention-getting" to the child. Spanking, Time Out, and grounding are forms of significant consequences. They get your child's attention. But if you have a defiant child, significant consequences usually aren't as effective as the other two in teaching your child the right behavior. The main purpose of significant consequences is to get your child's attention and, hopefully, make him pause the next time he begins to misbehave.

Consider one of Ray's clients: a ninth grader who refused to do homework or schoolwork and wound up failing school. Each week, his teacher sent a grade report home to show his parents whether he'd turned in all of his assignments. If he had missed even one assignment, his parents punished him by taking away all his privileges: talking on the phone, listening to his stereo, using the computer, watching television, and hanging out with his friends.

Since that didn't work over a period of several weeks, his parents then confined him to his room, which had only a bed, a bureau, a lamp, a bookcase, and a few essential things. He was only allowed out of his room for school, meals, and bathroom use. After a few days of this "solitary confinement," the boy's father walked into the boy's room to find him playing with a piece of aluminum foil that he'd molded into the shape of an army soldier.

Although you, we, and most other people in the world—including most children—would have folded after just a couple of hours of this significant consequence, this teenager was entirely unaffected. His parents were trying to coerce him into doing his homework, but the significant consequence they chose was resulting in absolutely no behavior change.

If you are going to use a significant consequence, find one that means something to the child. For this boy, a better choice would be to use manual labor—such as mowing the yard or taking out the trash—rather than Time Outs and taking away privileges. In other words, if one style of consequence isn't getting through to your child, try another.

If you don't know what would get your child's attention and motivate him to change, you might have to experiment to find out. Let's say that your child turns the TV on and off, over and over again, despite your persistent threats to take away his television privileges if he doesn't stop. He obviously isn't worried about watching the tube, or he wouldn't keep pushing your buttons. So you need to find something that is important to him—video games, his skateboard, or something similar—and take that away. You can't hand out a significant consequence without first discovering what is meaningful to your child.

An exemplary approach would be the one used on a boy named Gabe, who refused to do his schoolwork. Gabe didn't mind being spanked or being put into Time Out. Related and relevant consequences had no effect on him either. Parents and teachers became frustrated trying to figure out what could possibly get through to the boy until, one day, one of Gabe's teachers began to notice that the boy was extremely slow-moving and lazy. She noticed that Gabe was happy as long as he didn't have to move and could be still for long periods of time.

This teacher decided to experiment by making him do jumping jacks during lunch, recess, and other breaks.

And it worked! The child hated exercise so much that he was willing to do anything—including his schoolwork—to avoid the jumping-jack drill.

So, if no other form of consequence will work, make sure that you know precisely what will capture your child's attention before you give a significant consequence.

Working Through a Succession of Consequences

As we mentioned earlier in this chapter, the most effective consequence is a natural one. After that comes relevant, followed by related and—finally—significant. Here's how the sequence would play out in a real-life situation.

A good friend of ours, Joe Cates, is a principal at an alternative school in Plano, Texas. One day, Joe got a call from a teacher because a little first grader had been caught with his pants down, literally, exposing himself to a little girl.

Embarrassed once he was caught, the boy pulled his pants back up. The teacher called Joe and asked what an appropriate punishment would be. Joe asked the teacher how the child was responding to the past few minutes' activity, so the teacher looked down and reported to Joe, "The boy's crying." Joe asked the teacher what she was planning to

Major Types of Consequences

Consequences work better than punishments for leading your child toward appropriate behavior. Here are the key types of consequences, presented in their order of effectiveness from most effective to least effective.

1. *Natural consequences.* These consequences occur as a direct result of forces of nature (for example, if you don't eat, you get hungry). These can also include human emotional responses (for example, feeling embarrassed or ashamed). You can't give a natural consequence; you can only block it.

2. *Logical consequences.* Logical consequences occur when a human intervenes to impose a consequence. Example: If your child does not turn in his homework, he gets a "zero" grade.

Due to the difficulty that many adults have in selecting an *effective* logical consequence, we have further broken this concept down into three sublevels. These are again listed in order of effectiveness from most to least:

▶ *Relevant consequences* directly lead a child closer to the desired behavior. Example: making a child do the same homework assignment four times when he fails to turn it in.

▶ *Related consequences* have a relationship or kinship to the desired or problem behavior. Example: making a child spend the weekend in his room studying all of his school subjects when he fails to turn in his homework.

▶ *Significant consequences* are meant to get your child's attention, but they do not lead your child closer to the desired behavior, nor are they related to the problem behavior. Example: restricting your child's telephone privileges for failing to turn in his homework.

do with the child, and the teacher replied that she wanted to send the kid home. That wasn't the best tactic in this case.

Ashamed of himself, the embarrassed boy wanted to go home. Joe suggested instead that the child needed to experience his natural consequence by sitting in class. The boy's feelings were a natural consequence that helped him learn not to do that again because he didn't like being embarrassed and ashamed.

What if this youngster hadn't been embarrassed and had displayed bravado at exposing himself? Then sending him back to class would not have been a natural consequence and the behavior would likely have occurred again.

The next step for his teacher would have been to think of a relevant consequence. The desired behavior in that case would have been for him to keep his pants zipped while he was talking to his classmate. However, as you can see, this is a desired behavior that he does most of the time (similar to breathing clean air if caught smoking).

The teacher would then have gone to the next level of progression and tried to determine a related consequence. She could have had him discuss with the class the value of social appropriateness and the usefulness of clothes, but somehow that topic would probably have been lost on a first grader.

If she had gone through the logical steps of first a natural, then a relevant, and finally a related consequence, and she *still* hadn't come up with anything that had an impact, his teacher would have been left with the last choice: significant consequences.

If the child had not been embarrassed when caught exposing himself and if he had done it to get a reaction from the little girl or a laugh from his class, then separating him from his class, depriving him of the attention, or sending him home would have been the logical alternative, the significant consequence.

Knowing a child and watching his reaction is key to determining which consequence will be the best learning opportunity for him. Thinking in these logical steps will help you in determining which consequence to use.

Chapter 16

Time Out

Why a Little Chill Time
Can Be a Good Thing

*U*nless you've been locked in a room watching football games for the past 15 years, you probably know what kind of Time Out we're talking about. It does resemble an athletic Time Out; ideally it marks the end of action. Only with this type of Time Out, a misbehavior, rather than a sporting event, is interrupted.

We want to be perfectly clear: Time Out is a negative consequence because it will not teach your child how you want him to behave. Instead, he'll learn what results when he continues to misbehave, and he'll learn that you are in charge. Please remember, this punishment should not be delivered with anger. One purpose of Time Out is to correct the hierarchy of power in your home, and putting your child into Time Out with anger written all over you would defeat that purpose. (The other purpose of Time Out is to create a cooldown period for you and your child.)

132

Choosing the Time and the Place

Before starting Time Outs, the very first thing you need to do is settle on a place where the child will be during his punishment. This decision needs to be made when you are in a calm state of mind. This is not a good exercise to save for when the child is misbehaving and you are upset.

The best place to put your child would be a boring and bland place: a hallway, a dining room, a laundry room, or your bedroom—not at the dining room table with a clear view of the television. The child should face the wall, but not with his nose in the corner. We advise against putting your child in his own bedroom because he'll have too many toys and other interesting distractions. Besides, a kid's room should only be a safe haven for him and a place where he can chill out and then come out when he is ready. Going to his own room should be an intermediate step that your child can take to cool himself down.

When should you enforce a Time Out? That will vary. No one behavior or set of behaviors is an automatic trigger. Instead, consider following this general rule: If your child is physically aggressive or openly defiant, then he's telling you that he needs a Time Out so he can better understand who's in charge. The key thing is that the child should know that if he behaves defiantly, he will deserve a penalty.

How to Enforce a Time Out

Once a site has been determined and the child understands that his misbehavior can result in a Time Out, the next step is to follow through when the occasion arises.

Kids need boundaries, and they will likely test your borders soon after the rules have been set. It is important that your word be true. If your child is sent into Time Out for a violation but manages to weasel his way out of it, you have lost serious credibility with him. If you don't believe that this is true, think about the last time that you passed by a cop while you were speeding and he didn't pull you over. From that point on, you probably were tempted to think that you could get away with going a certain number of miles per hour over the limit without getting a ticket. It takes a long time (or a $200 speeding ticket) before you respect the law as much again. The same is true with your child and the "laws" that you set forth.

The way that you enact the punishment is critical too. You don't want your child to see Time Out as an unexplained penalty that *you* impose when *you're* angry; you want him to understand that *he's* done something inappropriate and *he's* responsible for the punishment.

Let's say that your defiant child hits his little brother. With sadness in your voice (though you may very well be angry), you say, "Uh-oh, Billy. You just earned a Time Out. Let's go." You put him into Time Out in the designated area.

The first time you put your child into Time Out, he should be there only as long as it takes for him to gain control over himself. You should tell him to sit in Time Out and come out when he can be respectful, play nicely with his brother, or reverse whatever behavior put him into Time Out. The one exception is if he has been very physically aggressive to you or someone else: Then, put him into Time Out for a designated period of time. This gives everyone time to cool off and provides you with an opportunity to attend to the injured person. Preferably, handle the injured person first, then put your child into Time Out.

We want your child to come out of Time Out on his own accord the first time, so that he will be thinking about what got him there and how he needs to act differently. This gives him some small amount of control over the situation. If he comes out of Time Out and his behavior has not improved or he remains disruptive, then the next time he goes into Time Out, he goes in under your conditions. What are those conditions? In order for him to get out, he must satisfy three standards:

1. He must do minimum time.
2. He must be quiet before you approach him—not throwing a tantrum or screaming.
3. Depending on his age, he must answer one of these questions:
   6 *and older:* "How do you plan to handle the situation differently next time?"
   Under 6: "Are you ready to pick up your toys?" or "Are you

ready to apologize to your brother?" or generally, "Are you ready to make amends for what landed you in Time Out?"

Let's look at these steps in a little more detail.

Minimum Time

Minimum time is 1 to 2 minutes per year of age, so a 6-year-old must be in Time Out for 6 to 12 minutes, minimum. We recommend that you determine whether to use 1- or 2-minute increments depending on how angry you are as an adult, not depending on the infraction. If *you* need a little more time to calm down, then take it. No child ever died from staying in Time Out for a few extra minutes.

If the child is 4 years old or younger, be a little more flexible and put him into Time Out for 2 to 3 minutes. Two to 3 minutes for a 4-year-old most likely feels like eternity.

A key point with this first condition is *minimum* time. Minimum time is 1 minute per year of age (unless your child is 4 or younger). Maximum time is until the child can qualify for Social Security, but hopefully none of us would hold a grudge that long, nor can we imagine that any child would misbehave for that long. The point is, don't think that if your child is still being sassy in Time Out, you have to let him out just because a certain amount of time has passed.

The record that we're aware of is held by a patient of Ray's who was in and out of Time Out for 4 hours. If you believe that your child is in Time Out too long, then you seriously need to consult a therapist because something else may be wrong or overlooked.

Getting back to minimum time, if after 3 minutes a 6-year-old announces to you that he is ready to get out, your response should be, "Thank you for sharing."

While your child is in Time Out, you want him to be quiet because this indicates that he has stopped feeling pure emotions and has started thinking about solutions. Before you approach your child, you want him thinking about new behaviors to engage in. You don't want him to still be blinded by emotions.

Way too often, adults approach children when they are still yelling, screaming, and emotional and try to talk reason into them. *This is a big mistake.* It is important to let your child calm down on his own time, which may not always be in your time frame.

Another mistake many parents make: They approach a child after the minimum time has elapsed and ask if he is ready to talk about getting out of Time Out, and the child says no. Rather than walking away, the parents start talking to the child about what is upsetting when, actually, the child needs more time by himself and is appropriately telling the parents that he needs more time. Please allow your child to stay in Time Out longer if he needs it.

Quiet Time

A child who is still saying nasty things or mumbling to himself is likewise telling you that he needs more time alone to come to terms with the consequence of his action. Imagine yourself as a waiter and your child as a valued customer at your restaurant: If he still had his menu open and was deciding what to eat, you wouldn't tap him on the shoulder and ask for his order. You would wait until he had folded the menu and appeared relaxed; then you'd approach him.

An Appropriate Response

What we mean by this third step—asking the child about his plan for next time—is that your child must have a plan in order to get out of Time Out. If he hit his little brother out of frustration, then, in order to leave Time Out, he must come up with a plan of how to handle his little brother and the situation differently next time.

This must be a *plan* and not a *wish* that something will happen on its own (without the kid's help). For example, in the scenario that we just described, if the child just says, "I'll be good and not hit him," that's a wish. A plan is a series of steps that he will follow either in his thoughts or through his actions. For example, your child might say, "Next time I get frustrated with Joey because he takes one of my toys, I will come get you and have you give the toy back." Don't allow your child to make a negative statement like "I won't hit him anymore" or a vague statement like "I'll be good." These are merely wishes.

What if your child comes up with a not-so-great plan that does not make a problem for anybody else? Then you should allow it. Imagine that your child says, "I'll go into my room and yell as loud as I can into my pillow." Even if you feel that that isn't a good way of handling his frustration, we recommend that you let him do it. The child is doing some good problem solving, and it is not important that he think the same way as you.

It's important for your child to have some latitude so he learns how to develop his own plans. And just because a child comes up with a plan doesn't mean that he is going to institute it. Actually, it is quite unlikely that he will employ his plan right after coming up with it. But you are getting him to do the thinking, which is the important part.

If you reach the third condition for leaving Time Out and your child is not yet 6 years old, phrase a question that can only be answered "yes" or "no." For instance, ask whether he's prepared to do what is required in order to get out of Time Out. "Are you ready to apologize to your little brother for hitting him?" "Are you ready to stop hitting Mom and apologize to me?" "Are you ready to pick up the living room instead of throwing the toys around?" or "Are you ready for an Academy now?" (We'll talk more about Academies in "The Academy," Chapter 20.)

If your child says yes, then let him out of Time Out. If your child says no or gives you some kind of response like "It's your fault," or if he sits there silently, then turn, walk away, and come back in 3, 4, or 5 minutes. *Do not* try to force the issue and make your child talk. You will end up with another power struggle that you will lose. Walk away.

After your child has satisfied this third condition, give him a hug to assure him that you won't hold any grudges and that Time Out is over. Or give him an acknowledgment the next time you notice that he's heading in the right direction, such as when he starts picking up a mess that he made. Either a hug or an acknowledgment (or both) will help your child realize that you are not going to hold any serious grudges and that he has a chance to begin repairing the damage done. It is very important for the child to hear or see something from you as an adult to realize that Time Out is over.

Warnings about Time Out

While Time Out is one of the more effective techniques available for parents and teachers, for several reasons it is also one of the most abused and misunderstood.

First, parents sometimes mistakenly send children to Time Out in places that aren't conducive to good thinking—for instance, we put them in their rooms for long periods of time. Once there, these kids usually just entertain themselves because there is usually more entertainment in a kid's room than at Epcot Center in Disney World.

Teachers, on the other hand, often put their children out in the hallway to serve Time Out. Ray entered one school and saw several children lined up in a hallway, waving at one another. Ray asked the guidance counselor what the children were up to, and she claimed that they were in Time Out. We consider that relocation, not Time Out.

One mother bitterly complained that Time Out wasn't working with her son. When her boy misbehaved, she placed him at the dining room table. All he did was stare into the next room and watch television from there. We don't consider that Time Out either. All she had done was move the boy one room away from the television, making it slightly harder for him to hear.

A second way that we adults misuse Time Outs is by applying them without first having a base of positive interactions with a child—the sorts of things we talked about building up in part 4. Your child should see Time Out as a negative consequence that takes him away from the positive attention that he craves.

Unfortunately, many children come to view Time Out as "Time Out from nagging, bitching, yelling, cajoling, whining, and complaining," which is how we adults often unwittingly use it. In reality, Time Out should mean "Time Out from positive stimulation and attention." That is, time away from something that your child likes or enjoys.

Think about the difference between how you'd react to a negative and a positive Time Out at work. If your boss nagged you and then put you into Time Out, he'd be releasing you from something you didn't like anyway. In a sense, this would be a relief for you. Conversely, if you were used to getting positive attention at work and your boss placed you in Time Out, he would be taking you away from something that you would miss.

Or, if we said to you, "That's it! Now you've done it. You've lost the privilege of using your limousine," you'd probably think, "So what? Take away my helicopter too. I don't have either one. So taking them away won't hurt me." In the same sense, a child who doesn't receive positive attention from adults isn't going to view a Time Out away from those adults as a useful punishment.

Another way that we adults can short-circuit Time Outs is by overusing them. If you rely on Time Outs too much, or if you use them every single time that the child misbehaves, they lose their power. Remember, Time Out is best used as a break from the action and as a time to think and regroup. It does not teach a child what he should be doing instead. As we mentioned in "The Power of Consequences" on page 127, Time Out is a significant consequence—not a relevant one. We urge you to look at Time Out merely as another option to curtail misbehavior, not as the *only* option.

In fact, we suggest that at first, you use Time Out only for a maximum of two misbehaviors—both of which, if possible, should be very specific and clearly outlined to the child ahead of time.

Some examples would be physical aggression or disrespectful language. Both of these behaviors are easy to track on what we call a video example. Remember, video examples are behaviors that your child could clearly see if you captured them on videotape. If you videotaped your child hitting his little brother and showed the tape to 10 people, they would all agree that your child was being aggressive. But if you told him that he was showing his brother "disrespect," that would be harder

BEHAVIOR BASICS

The Rules for Time Outs

Time Out can be an effective way to help your child modify his behavior if you keep four rules in mind.

1. Your child must do a minimum amount of time.
2. Your child must be quiet before you approach him.
3. When you approach him, he must answer one of the following questions:
   (a) 6 or older: "What do you plan to do to handle the situation differently next time?"
   (b) Under 6: "Are you ready to put away your toys?" or "Are you ready to apologize to your brother?" Ultimately, "Are you ready to make amends for the behavior that landed you in Time Out?"
4. Once your child gets up from Time Out, you should either give him a hug or acknowledge his next good behavior—or both.

for your make-believe viewers to see on a videotape. And if those make-believe viewers would be confused about what constitutes disrespect, you can be assured that your child will be also.

So, be very specific with your child about what constitutes bad behavior, and give him examples that he can visualize. You might tell him not to respond in a certain tone of voice, or something similar. This will help both you and your child.

Too often, parents and teachers issue Time Out when they are exasperated. In that case, it is a last-ditch effort rather than an opportunity for the child to learn. Even though Time Out is a "negative consequence," you can—and should—use it in a positive manner.

Hold Downs

What to Do When Your Child Won't Sit in Time Out

After reading the last chapter, many of you may be asking, "So what would you professionals do if a young child won't sit in Time Out . . . huh, guys?"

The answer is to "raise the stakes," and that's the focus of this chapter.

Time Out is wonderful. But, as many of you well know, not only do children not like it, they also often won't stay in Time Out. This is not the point where you should give up, though. Instead, it is important to help your defiant child understand who is running the show in your home or whatever environment he is in.

Parents and other adults should be the ones in charge, and children should not have free reign. When a child releases himself from Time Out without your permission, he is saying that he doesn't clearly understand that chain of authority. So you must let the child know that he is not in charge and that you don't mind using a stiffer consequence to handle the situation.

For a younger child whom you know you can restrain, the stiffer consequence that we recommend is a Hold Down—where you literally hold the child in Time Out against his will.

Before we get into the specific techniques, we would like to stress the importance of using Hold Downs as something of a last resort. If you turned to this chapter at random, please don't use it as an excuse to wrestle your child to the ground the next time he refuses to clear off the table. Part 5 of this book is written as a logical series of steps for restoring order to your household. We always hope that the lesser consequences outlined in "The Power of Consequences" (Chapter 15)—or even the Time Outs that we just discussed in Chapter 16—will strike a chord with your child and help him recognize your authority.

If those strategies aren't working, though, we highly recommend the appropriate use of Hold Downs. In all our years of prescribing Hold Downs for defiant kids, we have never heard of a case where a child sustained injury when the steps that we outline were followed properly. And in all those years, we have seen thousands of parents finally get through to their extremely strong-willed children by using these techniques.

Although Hold Downs are extremely effective, they should be used with caution and only after careful thought. Foremost, the Hold Down needs to be done in a manner in which your child cannot hurt himself or you. The illustration opposite shows the correct approach.

Also note that Hold Downs are not appropriate for every child or parent. (See "Warnings about Hold Downs" on page 145.)

If you decide to use Hold Downs as part of your parenting, use the technique only when a child refuses to follow your instructions for Time Out. You will know when a child refuses to follow your instructions when he's been ordered to Time Out and he responds by refusing to go to the Time Out location; when he gets up before the minimum time is up; or when he scoots out of the Time Out area. If any of these things occur, your child is signaling that he needs your assistance to sit in Time Out.

To hold down your child safely, sit behind him and draw him up between your legs. Cross your legs over his, then grasp his hands as shown and hold him against your body. Place your head between his shoulder and head to keep him from butting you. Also, keep your hands out of reach of his mouth. Holding down a child in this way confines him without harming him.

How to Conduct a Hold Down

It is best to perform a Hold Down in the Time Out corner, but a defiant child sometimes won't even go into Time Out. In that case, you have to hold him down wherever he is. That might be in the kitchen, the living room, or your bedroom. There is no need to drag the child into Time Out once you have grabbed him and are holding him down.

Although emotions are certain to rage in your heart when you conduct a Hold Down, you cannot allow the youngster to see anger. Your purpose is to provide limits for the child. If your child notices that you are angry when the punishment is inflicted, he will likely act out that anger on you or others.

As you can imagine, a child will not like being held down and will want to be let up and let go of. However, once a child is in a Hold Down, he must satisfy three conditions in order to get up.

1. The child must be held for minimum time.
2. The child must stop struggling before you let him go.
3. After serving the minimum time and ceasing to struggle, the child must answer yes to this question: "Are you ready to sit in Time Out by yourself?"

Minimum Hold Down time is approximately 30 seconds per year of age. For instance, a 6-year-old must be held for 3 minutes. If, after 1 minute, the child says, "Okay, you can let me up now. I'll sit in Time Out," your response should be, "Thanks for sharing." You do not let him up until the minimum time has passed.

Often, you will hear a child who is being held down scream, cry, or yell in order to retain whatever little independence he still has. This is okay; your goal is only to get the child to stop struggling and do as he is told.

Once he stops struggling, he is indicating that he understands and acknowledges the chain of command. At that point, he recognizes that you are in charge and that he isn't. This acknowledgment need not be stated verbally. By ceasing to struggle, he has made it clear.

If the child says anything besides yes when you ask him whether he is ready to go into Time Out, you continue to hold him. For instance, if the child refuses to answer, continues to struggle, or starts making demands, then you continue the Hold Down and wait another 3 to 4 minutes, or whatever time you set.

Once the child agrees to sit in Time Out by himself, his time there starts. (If he previously left Time Out without permission, his time starts over.) The child must remain in Time Out until he meets the three conditions for leaving that are outlined in "The Rules for Time Outs" on page 140. After Time Out, hug your child or find the

Warnings about Hold Downs

Hold Downs are trying on everyone's patience, and they can be very upsetting. Several situations can make a Hold Down worse than it needs to be. Most common is when the adult is angry at the child, or when the adult yells at the child and holds or squeezes him too tightly.

If you feel emotionally incapable of holding a child while remaining in a somewhat stable and calm state of mind, do not even attempt a Hold Down.

Also, do not try using Hold Downs with your child if *you* lack self-control, have attention deficit hyperactivity disorder yourself, are battling substance-abuse problems, generally struggle with anger management, or have physically or sexually abused a child in the past. Conducting a Hold Down under any of these circumstances will only make the situation worse, infuriate your child, and cause further problems. In addition, your relationship with the child will deteriorate.

Here are other situations that rule out Hold Downs:

1. When the child has been sexually abused in the past.
2. When, as an infant, the child was restrained in neonatal intensive care unit for more than a day.

    In both of these cases, Hold Downs might trigger a post-traumatic stress disorder reaction in these children. Instead of a Hold Down, immediately consult a therapist for alternatives.

3. When your child has a physical condition such as cerebral palsy, or any other physical limitation where muscle strength is compromised. In cases like these, holding a child down will probably cause the child's muscles to tighten up and he won't be able to relax them easily. Instead, it is better to hold your child facedown on the floor with his arms by his sides. This will prevent unnecessary injury.

If you are unsure of when, how, or whether to use a Hold Down, consult a therapist.

first situation possible to acknowledge—or praise—his next good behavior.

At first, defiant children commonly go from Hold Down to Time Out and back to Hold Down several times as they test adults. The first Hold Down is usually the most intense and longest for a child. That is, the child will scream and yell louder, struggle more, and retaliate longer than in later Hold Downs.

In our combined experience, we have found that children are—on average—held down from 45 minutes to an hour and a half the first time. So don't become concerned if your child needs to be held for a lengthy period of time. This does not mean that something is wrong or that Hold Downs are not working. It just means that your child really needs to experience a Hold Down on several levels before he can acknowledge your authority.

Hold Downs can be draining, so make sure that you do this on your time and at your convenience, when you have support and energy and you have had a chance to practice the technique. We recommend that you don't attempt a Hold Down if you're completely drained from work and don't have the energy for it. Best to walk away and wait for a time when you have all the mental and physical energy you need for this battle. If you're not sure that you can handle a Hold Down by yourself, get a spouse or close friend to assist you. And we recommend that you practice with a more cooperative child, your spouse, or a friend before attempting to hold down your defiant child.

Anticipating Your Child's Reactions

When you apply the first Hold Down, your child will almost certainly yell and scream. The most common thing to hear from the child is "I can't breathe!" If your son is screaming "I can't breathe!" at the top of his lungs, he is using more than the normal level of oxygen to maintain his shouting. He can breathe just fine despite his constant insistence that he cannot. But if you are legitimately concerned, go ahead and loosen your grasp a little.

Your child also may say some hateful things like "You're awful," "I'm going to kill you," "You're the worst mom [or dad] in the world," or "I hate you." Though some verbal jabs may strike a nerve, you should ignore them and focus on your mission. These statements are just hooks to get you to engage in an argument—nothing more. And your child will respect you more if you continue the Hold Down than if you give in to the cries.

Beyond words, your child may struggle ferociously and possibly with violence, thinking that you will give up and allow him to win if he puts up enough of a battle.

Eventually, however, your child will agree to sit in Time Out after the first Hold Down. Yet even after that monumental Hold Down, your defiant child will probably still need a Hold Down from time to time. The Hold Downs will most likely never again be as long or intense as the initial one, though, because your child has learned that you mean business.

A defiant child won't praise you for holding him down. Your praise will come in the form of your child's actions. The next time you put your child into Time Out and he refuses, he will not resist the Hold Down for long. When he gives in and goes into Time Out with a sad pout in his eyes, he is saying, "I understand now. When you say Time Out, you mean business." The silence and peace is your reward, and you can rest assured that your child loves you and respects you more than ever before.

Coping with Your Reactions

When you use a Hold Down on your child, you can expect to feel extremely upset and concerned that you may be hurting and emotionally scarring him. You may fear that your child will hate you after this.

First, remind yourself that you are offering your child structure and limits in a loving way. You are not hitting or beating your child; you are merely saying, "If you can't control yourself, I will help you gain control."

Also, remember that kids like control and limits because those things help them grow and develop. Very often after a Hold Down and subsequent Time Out, children become more obedient and loving. We can tell you that most children will hug you more and say more loving things following this experience.

Hold Downs are no fun for child *or* parent. But they can be extremely effective and one of the best techniques to realign the hierarchy in your house. Also remember that Hold Downs will be useless unless you have a good relationship with your child to begin with.

Concerns about Using Physical Restraint

Sometimes at workshops, parents and caretakers ask us, "Aren't you advocating violence?" No, we're not. We are simply telling you to restrain *your child's* inappropriate and violent behavior.

Just as the purpose of law enforcement officers is to preserve and restore peace, so your intention in a Hold Down is to restore peace to your home.

In the 20 or more years that we have used and recommended Hold Downs, we have never had a child get hurt.

Some children injure their parents, but never have any of our clients' parents sustained a more serious injury than a bruise. Children occasionally wiggle free, and that is when they might manage a head butt to your rib cage or a kick to your shins. You need to be aware that Hold Downs are not always painless procedures for you. They are, however, vital. Without speaking, you are telling your defiant child, "Look, I will help you stay in control if you can't be in control. We are going to start correcting the hierarchy right now. So go ahead and fight it all you want. Once you figure out that you don't like my solution, perhaps you'll come up with a better one on your own." In other words, "You solve it—or I will."

How Hold Downs Helped One Family

Nine-year-old Michael didn't believe in the adage "Misery loves company." His philosophy was more like "Misery loves miserable company."

If he was the slightest bit unhappy, Michael felt that it was his God-given right to make others in his life miserable. He saw nothing wrong with making a problem for others. His mother—a therapist herself—permitted this and set few limits on him for fear that it would somehow damage his self-esteem. But after living with his attitude for some time, even she admitted that things had to change, and she started family therapy with Ray.

During his first half-dozen meetings, Ray noticed that the balance of power was badly skewed in Michael's home. The father worked most of the time, and the mother was worried about Michael's emotional well-being. The result: Michael often called the shots, and the entire household revolved around the little boy.

Ray realized that an intense ordeal would have to erupt before the balance of power could return to Michael's parents. So Ray prepared the parents for this upcoming battle by explaining the process of Hold Downs and asking them to practice.

On the family's next visit, Ray greeted the parents by shaking their hands. When Michael walked up behind his parents, Ray extended a hand and greeted the young boy. But Michael just grunted and walked past, refusing to shake hands. Had this been the family's first session, Ray would have let the incident pass. But knowing the issues surrounding Michael, Ray decided that this would be a good place to help Michael start forming new habits.

"Come back here, Michael, and shake my hand," Ray said politely.

Reluctantly, Michael returned to the waiting room. Ray repeated the procedure of greeting Michael and offering him his hand. With no eye contact and a wet washcloth handshake, Michael grunted, "Hi."

"Uh-oh," Ray stated compassionately, "what you are telling me is that you need a Greetings Academy." (See "The Academy," Chapter

20, for more on this technique.) "You know, where you practice saying hello to people."

"Yeah, right," Michael responded with an eye roll.

"We won't be able to start the session until you can practice this," Ray maintained.

"Mom!" Michael yelled down the hall past Ray, "tell this retard to let me go!"

Ray consulted quickly with Michael's parents and told them that the session would be delayed for a while until their son had had a chance to practice the appropriate behavior. Both parents were fine with this, so they watched apprehensively to see how Ray would deal with Michael's obstinate behavior.

Once Michael realized that his parents weren't going to save him, he let out a sigh, gave in a bit, and agreed to practice. But after the second practice, he announced to Ray—as if he were handing down an edict—that he had practiced enough, and that would be the end of the Academy.

"Thanks for letting me know," Ray responded. "But you still haven't done this well enough, so let's keep on practicing."

"*Screw you!*" he screamed. "You're not my father."

Ray took a breath and said, "Sounds like you need to go to Time Out to settle down. Why don't you have a seat facing the wall and come out when you think you are ready to do this Academy."

"You're a retard! This is gay!" Michael said.

Calmly, Ray noted, "Sounds like you might need some help going to Time Out. Can you go by yourself or do you want your parents to help?"

Agitated, Michael pushed past Ray, entered his office, and sat down in Ray's chair.

This message of control was not lost on Ray, who turned to Michael's parents and said, "I think Michael needs you to assist him in going to Time Out."

Michael's mother turned to negotiate with her son, which Ray quickly stopped.

"Really, this is probably not a good time to rationalize and explain. Your son needs your help, so help him," Ray offered.

Mom got out of her chair and, with a submissive tone, requested that Michael go sit in Time Out against the wall. Again, Ray nudged her: "The time for negotiations has passed, and he needs help going into Time Out."

Ray then asked Michael's father to assist. As both parents went to put their hands on Michael, he abruptly got up and sat with his back against the wall.

"Unfortunately, Time Out is facing the other way," Ray announced.

"I'll sit like this!" Michael demanded.

Again, Ray instructed both parents to help the child sit the correct way. And again Michael, in his agitated state, started to struggle. Then, Ray instructed Michael's parents to hold him down. After a struggle, they put him in a Hold Down. Michael's agitation and anger climaxed. For the next 25 minutes, Michael struggled, yelled, cursed, spit, and told Ray that he was "the Devil."

Finally, Michael agreed to sit in Time Out correctly. Exhausted, he sat in Time Out correctly while his parents reclaimed their places on the couch. After only a few minutes, though, he once again turned around—an action that gave his parents and Ray the clear message that Michael still wanted to be the one making the rules and decisions.

Again, Ray instructed Michael's mother to put him in a Hold Down. While Michael struggled, cussed, and spit during this Hold Down, the intensity was noticeably less—as was the duration.

Once again, Michael was given the opportunity to sit in Time Out correctly. Instead, he scooted over to the opposite wall, stating that he would do Time Out there. His parents looked to Ray as if to ask whether they should allow Michael to sit as he was or make an issue of it.

"Nope," Ray relayed, "he is not the one making the call."

Again, his mother (whom Michael defied most) was asked to place him in a Hold Down. This one lasted over an hour, with Michael struggling most of the time. His parents had to take over for each other, much like tag-team wrestling.

After this ordeal, both Michael and his parents were exhausted. The boy was physically exhausted, while his parents were more psychologically spent. They worried frantically that Michael's self-esteem was irreversibly damaged and that their relationship with him was compromised.

The next day, Ray called Michael's mother to find out how the rest of the evening and the next day had gone. "He was very quiet in the car, but he behaved unusually well at home and was very loving at bedtime. Even this morning went fine," she noted with amazement.

At the next session, Ray went out to the waiting room to greet Michael and his parents. Both the mother and father came in shaking his hand. Michael again lagged behind, as was his custom. Ray was prepared to have a reenactment of the previous session, but instead, Michael walked up to Ray, looked him in the eye, smiled, shook his hand, and in the nicest possible tone said, "Hi, Dr. Ray!" The major conflict that Ray had anticipated was now passed.

The act of shaking hands politely may seem like a trivial point to do battle over, but Ray identified it as one of the few battles that Michael's parents were capable of winning at that point. Appropriate greeting skills were certainly not the biggest problem Michael struggled with. But Ray knew that if he could reenact any of Michael's struggles during a therapy session, he would be able to assist the parents through the process of correcting the chain of command in their house. Ray focused on a small behavior and allowed a battle to occur when it was convenient for the adults, not necessarily convenient for Michael.

Other Options

If you feel uncomfortable holding your child down, we recommend that you still do something else to let your child know that his misbehavior will not be tolerated.

One intervention might be to put the child in his room and hold the door closed so that he cannot get out. But you must expect that his room will be destroyed because, in his rage, he will likely break everything that is destructible.

Another strategy is to put the child outside and let him cool off there. This is very effective, especially for adolescents. Wherever they aren't, adolescents want to be. If they are grounded to the house, they want to be outside. If they are grounded outside, they want back in.

If an adolescent threatens to run away while he is outside, your response should be something like "Write when you get where you're going." We are not suggesting that you recommend that your adolescent run away—only that you not let your child hold you hostage.

Hold Downs vs. Talking

To let a defiant child know that you are in control, you usually have to do something physical such as a Hold Down, or confining the child to his room, or putting him outside—anything that lets him know that his misbehavior will not be tolerated.

Trying to solve the issue by *talking* and *reasoning* at this point will most likely cause problems to worsen. Talking will give the defiant child the false impression that he is in control, and it will decrease your authority as a parent.

Plus, both of you are usually emotional at a time like this, which

BEHAVIOR BASICS

Four Rules for Conducting a Hold Down

1. *Make sure that you know when not to use a Hold Down.* Hold Downs aren't for everyone.
2. *Be prepared.* Figure out how your child might react to a Hold Down, and make a plan to offset his reaction.
3. *Check out your other options.* If a Hold Down isn't going to work in your case, choose another method for taking control.
4. *Follow through.* Before releasing your child from a Hold Down, make sure that he meets these conditions: serves minimum time, stops struggling, and states a willingness to sit in Time Out.

makes it hard to talk rationally. If you do not feel comfortable with a Hold Down or confining the child to his room, we strongly recommend that you walk away. Leave the situation and even the house, if necessary; but *do not* try talking your child out of his tantrums. That would only aggravate the problem and increase the likelihood of more tantrums.

With noncompliant children, there will be battles. You are most likely to win these if you fight on your terms. There will be times when you'll think to yourself, "Bag it! It is not worth struggling with him. I'll let his aggressiveness go this time." But as parents we cannot allow children to get away with misbehavior when we have the energy and support to fight it.

Moreover, Hold Downs are a consequence that kids don't like, so they will be more likely to come up with their own solutions to avoid another Hold Down. That's a benefit to you and to them.

Guided Compliance

Using Hands-On Training to
Encourage Your Child to Obey

Once Time Outs and Hold Downs have helped your child realize that you are ultimately in control, you can then work on raising his willingness to comply while limiting his arguing. For defiant children under the age of 9, an effective method is Guided Compliance.

This technique not only teaches the child to obey quickly but also trains parents not to repeat themselves or constantly nag the child, both of which clearly lose their effectiveness over time. Guided Compliance also helps train children's obeying skills.

To use Guided Compliance, you need to follow four steps.

Step 1. Begin with a simple command that your child needs less than 15 seconds to accomplish. It could be something like "put these forks on the table" or "pick your ball up off the floor." The command need not be something that you actually need to have done at that moment. Instead, consider this a training exercise.

The command should be direct—not a request. Remember, you are telling your child what to do; you are not asking. If you ask, your child will often give an answer that you won't like. If you say, "Johnny, would you come here and help me set the table?" Johnny's response might be "No." In that case, he would be responding appropriately to your question but not cooperating with you.

Also, don't ask rhetorical questions; just make statements—only try not to sound like Clint Eastwood in *Dirty Harry* by demanding that your child obey. Finally, make the command brief and don't give multiple commands. Remember, you are training both your child and yourself. So give the child something easy to do, like, "Joey, hand me the salt."

Step 2. If your child complies, praise him for obeying. But be careful not to go overboard. For example, you can say, "Nice job. Boy, you're really listening!," but you don't have to alert the media or jump up and down, because that will look fake to your child. If your child does not follow your command, however, you move to step 3.

Step 3. If your child does not begin to follow the command within 5 seconds, then physically guide him through the command. Do not count to five out loud first. That is simply giving the child a warning. Instead, repeat the command with the exact same wording and tone. For example, "Joey, hand me the salt." As you repeat the command, walk over to your child and physically place your hands on his arms and guide him through the action you've requested. For example, help him wrap his hand around the salt and bring him and the salt over to where you were sitting.

Step 4. After guiding him through the command, compliment the child. It may seem wrong to compliment your child after practically forcing him to behave, but you need to. The only difference between your initial command and the second time is that you are physically guiding the child. (That's where we get the term *Guided Compliance*.) He is still doing what you asked him to. So whether the child behaves on his own or with your help, give him a compliment. That will entice him to do things right the next time. "You solve it, or I will": Get it?

This new policy may shake your child up a bit since you're complimenting him even though you're doing all the work while he's merely acting like a puppet. It will cause a struggle in the child's head, leaving him thinking, "Hey, I don't want Mom to touch me, and I'm going to do whatever I can to keep her from touching me and making me do what I don't want to do. I'll even do what she's asking me to do."

Clearly, this is what you want in the first place. But you must allow the child to figure out how complying benefits him. Eventually he'll understand two things. First, he must obey, and he can either do it voluntarily or involuntarily. Second, if he complies on his own, he remains in control. That's a major incentive for strong-willed children, who do not like giving up their control.

Practicing Guided Compliance

When using this technique, you must continue making simple commands throughout the day and if necessary follow up with Guided Compliance. Figure on doing at least 20 commands per day. But remember that kids catch on quick. We don't recommend that you go through all the commands at once because your child will figure out what's going on. If he knows what you're doing, he will comply for a set amount of time and then stop complying on other occasions when you make requests.

Rather, you should attempt a couple of Guided Compliances the first time you use the method, then wait 10 to 20 minutes, or even an hour or two. Then try a few more, scattering the process throughout the day.

It is important that you only try Guided Compliance training when you are prepared to follow through. If you use the technique once or twice and then ignore your child's defiance after that, he won't understand the inconsistency. When you aren't able to make Guided Compliance work, do your usual nagging or cajoling or whatever it is that you have done in the past to get the child to comply.

A Case Study in Guided Compliance

Neal was the expert at selective attention. A 5-year-old, he could control and manipulate his mother, forcing her to repeat herself until she wound up screaming. Neal's mother even got his hearing checked, but she already knew that he was fine since he heard what he wanted to.

Accepting that Neal was voluntarily ignoring her, she decided to try Guided Compliance. Neal, who sat in on the therapy session where Ray explained Guided Compliance, watched closely that first night for his mother to robotically make simple commands of him.

"I knew she was doing it," Neal later told Ray. In fact, the mother reported that Neal followed her commands well that first evening and that she only had to guide him once.

The next day was a different story. Involved with his Lego blocks, Neal heard his mother's request to come to her and stated that he would, but instead feigned an early onset of Alzheimer's disease and quickly forgot, choosing instead to play. As soon as he felt his mother's hands on him, he became upset.

Then, after his mother had helped him get up and go where she'd asked him to, she began to praise him. Boy, was he ever confused. Where was the yelling he had come to expect? Where were the five to seven repetitions that his mother usually engaged in?

Later that night, Mom made another request, and in his usual style Neal ignored her. As she repeated it, he felt her hands on him again.

"Hey, lay off!" he demanded.

"Sweetie, if you don't listen the first time, I'll help you." Mom responded. "If you don't want me to touch you, you know what you need to do."

"Just don't touch me!" he demanded.

With the next command, Neal followed his mother's orders. Later that night, when Mom was putting him to bed, he announced proudly, "I know how to make you leave me alone."

"How?" his mother asked, taking the bait.

"If I just do a few things you ask, then you don't get to make me!" Neal smirked.

"Smart boy," said his mother with a smile.

What to Do When Your Child Struggles

Many children will not automatically go along with Guided Compliance. They will most likely respond like Neal by saying, "Hey, you can't touch me! Get away from me!" Then these children will normally do one of two things: They will passively resist by going limp (the "wet washcloth" response), or they will actively retaliate by digging in their heels and trying to physically resist you.

If either condition occurs, you should respond immediately by calmly saying, "Oh, how sad. I guess you just decided to go into Time Out." Then, you must immediately place the child into Time Out.

Now you can see why we discussed Time Outs and Hold Downs before getting to this point. To effectively change your defiant child's behavior, you have to work in steps. You cannot do Guided Compliance before you and your child have experienced and accomplished Time Outs and, if necessary, Hold Downs.

Keep the Monkey on Your Child's Back

Defiant children must know that most of the time you mean business when you request something of them, and it is their job to figure out when you want instant compliance and when they can delay and dawdle. There may be times when you ask your child to clean his room but you're not worried about it being done right away. But if you have company coming over in a few hours, he must understand that your voice is much more serious and he has to respond quickly. While your child figures out whether or not you want instant compliance, the struggle is between him and the figurative monkey on his back— not between you and him. Inside his mind is where the struggle should be.

When Guided Compliance is implemented properly, we've noticed that it has an extremely high success rate. Many parents report feeling more confident in making commands and requests of their children.

BEHAVIOR BASICS

The Four Steps of Guided Compliance

Guided Compliance is a technique that helps your child respond appropriately to your commands. It involves the following four steps.

Step I: Begin with a simple command, something that the child needs less than 15 seconds to accomplish.

Step 2: If your child complies, praise him for obeying.

Step 3: If your child does not begin to follow the command within 5 seconds, then physically guide him through the command.

Step 4: Finally, after guiding him through the command, compliment the child as if he had completed the command voluntarily.

Guided Compliance helps the child to understand that he must think for himself if he wants to retain some element of control.

Guided Compliance works well with children from ages 3 to 9. We don't recommend that anyone try to physically guide a 15-year-old into taking a plate from the dining room table to the sink. That could end with some nasty fights and awful aggression.

Use your own judgment. If you feel that the child can be physically guided safely, then give it a try. If you run into problems and experience no success, once again, we recommend that you try one of the other techniques we've explained in this book, evaluate whether you have a solid relationship with your child, or consider consulting a mental health professional.

Pulling In the Reins

How to Uses Choices to
Shut Down Arguments

A common complaint among parents and teachers is that children argue with them all the time about everything. But what adults sometimes fail to realize is that they are adding to the argument mix. Children only argue with adults who take the bait. Remember in "Avoiding a Power Struggle" when Ray argued with his daughter about wearing shoes outside?

Even if you remain perfectly quiet, though, there will be times when your child will continue a one-sided argument. This chapter explains what we recommend that you do during those annoying times.

As we've mentioned, the key to changing a defiant child is to train both the child and yourself. That is especially important to keep in mind when dealing with arguing. When a defiant child wants to argue or negotiate some privilege over and over again, adults tend to use reasoning, explanations, or defending. That can unwittingly intensify the child's defiant behaviors.

Instead, your best approach is to limit the amount of the problem you are causing. With Pulling In the Reins, you give the child choices and encourage appropriate actions. You also teach your child that he has a choice. He can behave and not argue, or he can lose his freedom and control, two things that are very important to him. Either he solves the problem or you will.

Pulling In the Reins in Your Home

There are three steps to using the Pulling In the Reins technique. To perform them effectively, you must rehearse them with your spouse or another adult and be ready to implement each one as the situation calls for it. Let's look at the specific steps.

Step 1. When your child is arguing with you, begin by giving him a choice with wide parameters and very few limits on it, such as "please either stay here and be quiet or argue about that point all you want someplace else in the house."

An example of a step 1 situation might be that your child tries to negotiate or argue with you over something like going to a convenience store for a candy bar 10 minutes before dinnertime. Even after you say no, the child continues to argue.

In the past, when you reached this point, you might have yelled, "What part of 'no' do you not understand?" But with Pulling In the Reins, you respond differently. You don't yell, you don't banish him to his room. You simply give him choices that have wide boundaries: He can go somewhere else in the house to complain if he chooses. Or if he wants to stay around you, he can change the subject or stop complaining.

This response shuts down the behavior that you don't want to see around you, while keeping you from getting caught up in your child's attitude. Most important, it sends your child a message: He is not misbehaving by complaining; his behavior is just misplaced, so he needs to behave that way someplace else.

Remember, trying to cajole him out of his bad mood usually doesn't work and often worsens his mood and outlook. Don't try the impossible. Once he is making better decisions, his outlook and mood will improve.

Step 2. If your child continues to argue and complain (which you can probably count on), do not repeat the original choices. Instead, take the best option away from him and replace it with a less preferable choice.

The best option in the earlier example was to stay in the same room with you and either stay quiet or change the subject. Since he continued arguing, though, you would now take that option away and, with sadness in your voice, say: "Oh, what a drag. Feel free to complain all you want someplace else, or go to your room."

Now, you have again given the child a lot of space to be in, such as the whole house minus where you are.

Most children who say no once will say it a second time and possibly a third and fourth. Your child will likely continue complaining, saying things like "You're so mean," "I hate you," "Wait till Dad hears about this," "I won't do my homework; I'll get you back."

Don't let the response get to you. Your child is just trying to engage you in an argument. Instead, just take away another choice and offer two other options, again taking away the most attractive option. For example, in a soft voice and with sadness in your voice, say, "Okay, you can go to your room or go to Time Out. Which one would you prefer?"

What is the child learning? Unless he makes a choice, you will make the choice for him. Defiant kids do not like other people making choices for them. This is a very valuable lesson, and they will figure it out, believe it or not.

Step 3. If your child continues to struggle, offer one final choice: "Do you want to go to Time Out by yourself or with my help?" At this point, you must follow through. Otherwise, you will only be saying that your word is no good.

As the child goes to Time Out, his first thought will be, "Hey, this is not fair! What happened to the old pattern of you arguing with me? What happened to that struggle where we'd fight for 10 minutes or more?"

Expect your child to be quite upset and unwilling to go into Time Out, in which case you must raise the stakes all the way by putting him into a Hold Down, if that's an appropriate response for a child his age. Again, this will help your child learn that if he doesn't make a decision, you will make the decision for him. But as we have stated throughout the book, it's important to let him figure that out. Don't take the pride of learning this lesson away from him.

After Pulling In the Reins a few times, you will probably notice your child acting more quickly to make better choices and prevent you from making them for him. Nothing gets under a defiant kid's skin more than someone else making choices for him.

How Pulling In the Reins Worked for One Family

"I'm going to Philip's house. Drive me now!" Mark demanded.

"Have you finished your homework?" Mom inquired. Mark, age 11, and his mother argued most nights over when he was going to get his homework done. Homework completion had always been a problem for him. On this night, Mom decided that the cycle needed to end. She had recently heard about Pulling In the Reins, so she put it into play this way.

MARK: *Why can't I go to Philip's? You are being such a bitch!*

MOM (BITING HER TONGUE): *Feel free to talk about that anywhere else or stay here and be quiet.*

MARK: *You never do anything for me. Yesterday, you were driving Corey [Mark's younger brother] all over the city. You act like he is the perfect child.*

MOM (TAKING AWAY THE BEST CHOICE): *Feel free to talk about that anywhere else or go to your room.*

MARK: *Go to my room? You're not my boss! Why won't you take me to Philip's? That's not fair!*

MOM (TAKING AWAY THE BEST CHOICE AGAIN WITH A CALM VOICE): *You can either go to your room or go to Time Out. What is your choice?*

MARK: *This is a free country. This is my house too. You don't have the right to tell me what to do!*

MOM: *Would you like to go to Time Out by yourself, or do you need my help?*

BEHAVIOR BASICS

How to Pull In the Reins

1. When your child is arguing with you, begin by giving him a choice with wide parameters and very few limits on it.
2. If your child continues to argue and complain, do not repeat the original choices. Instead, take away the best option and replace it with a less preferable choice. Continue to remove choices after each attempt by your child to argue or complain.
3. If your child continues to struggle, offer one final choice: "Do you want to go to Time Out by yourself or with my help?"

MARK: *This is retarded! I'll go to my room, so I don't have to put up with my retarded mother.*

MOM (AS SHE IS WALKING OVER TO HIM): *That wasn't a choice.*

MARK: *Don't touch me!*

Since his mother had previously gone through Time Outs and Hold Downs with him, Mark knew that his mother's word was good, and he wanted to avoid a Hold Down at all costs. So he took the last choice available to him and put himself into Time Out.

Consequences for Misbehavior

We have now discussed several ways that you can help your child make better decisions and end the power struggles. The Time Out, Hold Down, Guided Compliance, and Pulling In the Reins techniques do not work all the time, nor do they always work on every child. But overall, we have found these techniques to be effective in helping children become better problem solvers. Combined with the new techniques in the next chapter, they will make your child's compliance soar.

The Academy

What's the Key to Better Behavior?
Practice, Practice, Practice

Sammy Greene's eyes were closed in quiet sleep. His face appeared so relaxed. His 10-year-old body lay blissfully still.

To Karen Greene, her son looked very much like an angel. She savored this tranquil, serene moment almost every night. If only the calm of Sammy's sleep time carried through to the next morning.

It never seemed to work out that way, though. Come the dawn, Sammy was sure to start another storm. His little sister Melissa might be cheerful and cooperative, but not Sammy. *Every* morning, with his defiant attitude, he managed to turn what should have been a simple exercise of getting ready for school into an all-out battle.

He'd fight with Mom over getting out of bed and what to wear. He'd argue about what she wanted him to eat. He'd waste time torturing the cat. And no amount of pleading, cajoling, or screaming by Karen could change the way Sammy acted.

By the time that Karen finally got Sammy ready each day, he and his sister were often late for school, and Mom, as usual, was late for work. After months of this, Karen began to wonder if things would ever get better.

Rehearsing Good Behavior

Kids with defiant attitudes like Sammy's can be a real test. They make you wonder whether there is anything you can do to change their bad behavior. In fact, we've found a very successful way to deal with kids like this: Put them through an Academy.

As the name implies, an Academy is a formal way of training your defiant child to replace his bad behavior with actions you approve of. When a defiant child refuses to do something, he's telling you that he needs practice in that skill. That's what an Academy provides. It helps your child learn a proper behavior by practicing it over and over and over and over again. It's much like the way a math teacher might have students practice their multiplication tables until they get them right.

There are four major steps in an Academy.

> ► First, you explain to your child that his behavior is telling you that he needs help changing the way he acts.
> ► Second, you pick a time to conduct a practice—if possible, making it a convenient time for you and an inconvenient one for him.
> ► Third, you have your child practice the behavior you want—repeatedly.
> ► Fourth, when the Academy is over, you tell your child that he's done a nice job and casually announce that if any problems arise tomorrow, he will be telling you that he needs more practice.

Here's how the process works if, say, your child fails to perform a certain task: feeding the dog. When he refuses the job, you look at your child sadly and say, "Uh-oh. What your behavior is telling me is that you need a Dog-Feeding Academy." Try to say those words as calmly as possible, emphasizing that your child is sending this message through his behavior. Otherwise, the child will think that you are punishing with anger.

Next, you pick a time for the Academy. If it's convenient for you, great. But most important, it needs to be an *inconvenient* time for your child. An opportune time might be when your child is planning to go skateboarding with friends.

When the right time comes, say, "Okay, honey. Now it's time to practice feeding the dog." At this point, you instruct your child to sit on the living room couch. When you say, "Go feed the dog," he needs to get the dog's bowl, fill it with Kibbles 'n Bits, put it outside, change the dog's water, and go sit back down on the couch. You monitor each step.

If your child does everything adequately, you can say, "All right. That was done well." If that's the case, you have him undo the entire procedure: Put the Kibbles 'n Bits back in the bag, put the feed dish away, and sit back down on the couch. Then, once again, you say, "Charlie, it's time to feed the dog." He has to complete the entire procedure again.

We recommend that you redo the procedure in an Academy at least five to seven times—more if your child seems to be botching some part of it. What you want is to repeat it enough times to get some indication that your child is bored with the Academy—that it has become an ordeal.

Breaking It into Smaller Pieces

In some cases, you may need to break an Academy down even further to help the child understand every step. For example, you may be a teacher whose students have a hard time moving from the classroom into a cafeteria. You could break that down into these smaller components:

1. Getting out of the chair quietly;
2. Pushing the chair into the desk;
3. Walking in a straight line out the classroom door;
4. Walking down the hall quietly and in a single-file line;

5. Stopping as soon as the first child reaches the cafeteria door;

6. Entering the cafeteria;

7. Sitting down at a table.

You can have a student practice each component at your signal until he has the entire procedure down and can do it without fault. That means that you could have the child do the first step, then start over with the first step followed by the second step, then start over with the first step and the second step and add the third, and so on until the whole procedure is complete.

You can do this with more than one child at a time. Let's say that you have five children struggling with this issue. Ask those five to stay in class during recess to practice "going to lunch."

Yes, There Will Be Complaints

We can warn you right now that there will be anguish when you first introduce your child to Academies. He may need to retrace the same steps a dozen times. This will be difficult for you. You may have to bite your tongue to refrain from lashing out with obscenities. Your child is not the only one affected by the Academy.

But we can guarantee that if you stay the course, eventually your child will get it down. Eventually, after he has repeated the appropriate behavior time and again, something will snap, and your child will realize, "Oh yeah, this isn't so hard!"

That's the way it worked for Sammy Greene, the boy we mentioned at the beginning of this chapter. In his case, Ray recommended that Sammy's mother focus the first Academy on getting ready in the morning. Karen agreed.

So, one night after dinner, the Academy kicked in: Sammy finished eating on schedule at 7:00 P.M. and then began to head into the living room to watch his favorite show. His mother stopped him cold and told him that it was time for him to practice waking up in the morning.

"No way," Sammy barked. "I'm not doing that stupid thing and missing my show."

His mother responded coolly: "Either you can practice or you can go sit in Time Out until you are ready to practice. If you practice now, we can get it all done in probably about 45 minutes."

After a lengthy Time Out, Sammy realized that his mother meant business. Eventually, he did as he was told. He climbed the steps, put on his pajamas, set his alarm, turned out the lights, and climbed into bed. A moment later, the alarm sounded. A moment after that, Karen came up and told him that it was time to get up. So Sammy had to get out of bed, brush his teeth, dress himself, and go downstairs for breakfast.

He struggled with his mother a little but eventually completed the routine once, then headed back to the living room to catch the end of his show. Again his mother stopped him.

"No," she said. "We need to do it at least five times tonight."

After another Time Out, Sammy completed the next practice—but with a poor attitude. Like a coach whose basketball team ran a sprint halfheartedly, Karen coolly explained that that practice didn't count. Not only did Sammy need to go through the motions, but his whole outlook also had to improve.

Despite that first evening's ordeal, Sammy was still sluggish and dawdling the next morning. After the second and third nights of practice, Karen began wondering whether she would ever see any results.

But on the fourth morning, Karen turned from the stove and almost dropped her breakfast bowl on the floor. There sat Sammy—right next to his father—all dressed for school. She had not even climbed the stairs to badger him to get up! As he sprinkled salt onto his scrambled eggs and took a sip of milk, Karen saw the results of all her hard work.

Why Academies Work

Have you ever watched a marching band perform? The very best bands amaze us with their straight lines, deft maneuvers, and flawless harmony. Each instrument seems perfectly in tune with the others, and all 200 members appear connected by some invisible string.

If you've never witnessed the long, tense hours that those musicians spend practicing, you might assume that they just have a knack for harmonizing and marching together. But the truth is, many of those band members started out as clumsy as Barney Fife from *The Andy Griffith Show*. Patient band directors showed them how to work together properly. They spent grueling hours repeating the same steps over and over. Dozens of band members broke down and cried—sometimes even the director shed tears—as everyone tried to get it right.

Retracing those same steps over and over—and over again—gets old. So does playing the same notes, hearing the director bark out the same instructions, and watching fellow band members screw up on the same sequences. But on the night of the big performance, the result of all that careful repetition pays off. The performers sound so sweet and their intricate patterns look so easy to those of us in the stands that we cheer, we marvel at the perfection. We may even get goose bumps.

Just as practice works for the marching band, it can work for your child. And when it does, you may get goose bumps too. Also remember that the practice we are talking about in this chapter is not punishment. The band director doesn't make his students repeat the same moves and songs to punish them. He's just trying to help them learn. That's all you are trying to do.

One other point to note: Academies not only help your child function today, they also prepare him for tomorrow. In the real world, adults have to learn how to deal with frustrations, rigidity, sensitivities, and insensitivities in order to manage a decent living. And as a parent, you want to help your child develop the skills to do those things as well.

Lacking in the Social Graces

Many child therapists believe that defiant kids do not possess certain skills, and that this lack of skills directly causes them to be difficult. These therapists believe that if the kids could behave and comply, they would.

We have found that some defiant kids actually *do* lack some skills. They don't seem to know how to handle situations appropriately. They often lash out at others and have "meltdowns" where they completely lose their tempers. If you have a child like this, you may just think that he's spoiled because he wants what he wants when he wants it— entirely on his time frame.

The Man Who Founded the Academy

Joe Cates, a friend of Ray's to whom we've referred occasionally in earlier chapters, serves as the principal of an alternative school outside of Dallas. Not a place for the timid of spirit or meek of heart, this school houses the most deviant, devilish public school students in the area.

During the mid-1990s, Ray dropped by Joe's school to check on a client. He prepared for the loud cursing, yelling, and violence that certainly awaited him inside. He expected students to be wearing black T-shirts advertising their favorite rock or rap bands, and he expected graffiti on the walls and unkempt teachers frantically trying to restore order.

Ray opened the door—and almost stopped to ask a nearby janitor if he was at the right place.

The floors were freshly waxed, the lockers and walls were free of vandalism, and the staff seemed remarkably free of stress as they walked the halls. The place looked very much like a model high school or junior high.

Joe met Ray at the office entrance and Ray had to ask: "How have you made all these kids behave so well?"

Joe just shrugged his shoulders and said, "We just have them practice behaving. Most schools have students practice their times tables, and they require basketball players to practice their jump shots. But they usually don't have them practice behaving."

How simple.

But oh, how brilliant!

In the 5 years since Ray first tried this with his own clients, he has seen order restored to literally hundreds of homes and classrooms—all by practicing this commonsense strategy of repeating the right behavior over and over again. Ray has taken the Academy concept and developed a few extra twists to make it even more effective. But the original idea came from Joe Cates for a very basic reason: He wanted to help kids learn how to behave.

But these kids really aren't spoiled. They truly have difficulty knowing how to act appropriately, especially when their emotions are involved. It is not uncommon for them to have full-blown meltdowns over relatively small things, like having a pencil knocked off their desk accidentally by another child or getting a sandwich that wasn't cut the "right" way. We consider these children as having a *skills deficit*. They simply have not developed the skills to perform appropriately in many situations. These children respond to—and profit from—Academies because this approach directly teaches them how to act and behave.

Academies are a consequence that leads children toward the appropriate behavior. Academies don't punish them for acting up. These inflexible children will usually come across as appreciative after being led through an Academy: Before the Academy, they had no clue how to handle a situation; now, they do.

Defusing the "Explosive Child"

Some kids clearly have skills deficits and are extremely inflexible in a number of settings—even more so than other defiant children with skills deficits. Ross Greene, Ph.D., talks about these children in his book *The Explosive Child*. More than other children, these "explosive" kids need and benefit from Academies.

After these inflexible children do an Academy, they often are happier because they know how to act and react in situations where they previously didn't know how to behave. In our experience, children like this often like the Academy and thank their parents or teachers for helping them master the behavior.

Take the case of Steven, a child who was almost expelled from the second grade for aggression and for hitting his fellow classmates. He honestly didn't know how to respond correctly to classroom rules. One such rule had to do with play stations, areas sprinkled throughout the classroom where children could play with Lego blocks, crafts, puzzles, or other educational toys. The rule was that only two children were allowed to be in any one station at a given time.

Steven would often walk up to the Lego center, see two children already there, and become frustrated and confused. In his frustration, he usually hit one of the two children.

Upset, the assaulted child would leave to get the teacher. But through Steven's eyes he'd solved the problem, because once the injured child left, there was only one child in the Lego center and he could enter.

To help Steven, Ray set up a scenario in his office that was similar to the one in school. He told Steven to reenact what happened at school as closely as possible. Ray was playing with the Lego blocks when Steven came up and asked to play along with him.

"Get lost, booger boy!!!!" Ray stated provocatively.

Steven just stood there, lost, not knowing what to do.

"What are you going to do now," Ray inquired, "hit me?"

Steven shook his head no but still stood there, befuddled.

"What other options are there for you, Steven?" Ray asked.

"I don't know," responded Steven, while wearing a look of bewilderment.

"Could you go play in another center?" Ray suggested.

Right at that moment, Ray could see a lightbulb come on in Steven's head. This boy had literally never thought of that option.

After Steven went to another center to play, Ray had Steven reenact that scenario several more times as part of the Academy. After this simple training, Steven was never aggressive during center time again, and after two Academies for playground aggression, Steven's violence in school was almost nonexistent.

Clearly, Steven had a skills deficit, and his lack of mental flexibility made it more difficult (but not impossible) for him to automatically know the appropriate behavior.

Academies are also effective in helping children with more severe problems, including those who have been diagnosed as being emotionally or psychologically disturbed. Sometimes, parents and teachers will refuse to address problem behaviors with a child like this because they fear that it will "push the child over the edge." We haven't found that to be the case. We also believe that, in the long run, backing away from treatment disables the child since no one believes that he is capable of improving and no one holds him accountable. (*Note:* You should *not* use Academies if your child has been diagnosed with bipolar disorder or some other severe mental disorder. When in doubt, consult a therapist for advice.)

Using Academies to Change Attitudes

The Academy technique can be used to resolve a wide variety of inappropriate behaviors. For Corey, the problem was his attitude toward his sister. Corey's parents complained that the boy was unnecessarily rude and critical of his sister at dinner. He was very attentive in a negative way: He paid close attention to her every word and move during meals and would point out any poor manners. According to this young boy, everything would be just fine if only his younger sister had never been born.

The parents, meanwhile, were bitterly frustrated because dinner was always a stressful time in their household. Telling Corey to ignore his sister did absolutely no good. The little boy had a diagnosis of Asperger's syndrome, a developmental disorder characterized by poor social skills, communication difficulties, and an inflexible thinking style.

Ray suggested that Corey's parents start up a Politeness Academy to help the youngster comprehend how to act properly at the table. So, each day, after Corey got home from school—a time when he used to play with friends—Mom sat down with him at the dining room table. In his sister's chair, Mom propped up a rag doll. Corey had a plate and glass in front of him, just as he would during a meal.

During the practice dinner, Corey practiced looking at everyone in his family—not just his sister—and he could only make nice remarks. The Academy lasted for 20 minutes the first day. After one Academy, Corey claimed that he got it and needed no more help, and he appeared to enjoy the practice.

In fact, to his mother's surprise, Corey actually appreciated the practice. He didn't have politeness skills and he liked the fact that his mother was helping him develop them.

That night at dinner, he acted appropriately pleasant and kind. But he started in on his sister the very next evening. His mother—never missing a beat—said, "Corey, sounds like you're telling me that you need more practice. We'll practice tonight after dinner."

Realizing that his favorite show came on after dinner, he wailed: "No Mom! Please, no!" Unfortunately, Corey had to miss his show because he needed 30 minutes of practice that night (funny coincidence). Corey's behavior at dinner improved significantly for 10 days. Then, during a family night of dining out, he tried his antics again. And once again, his mother held a practice Academy at home at a time when Corey had planned to go over to a friend's house.

That was the end of Corey's dinnertime rudeness.

Academies for the Older Child

You might think that a process like this would be appropriate only for younger children, but it works remarkably well with older ones too.

One mother was having problems getting her teenage son to clean up the kitchen after himself. After school and most evenings, he would snack (or "hog," as his mother would refer to it) and leave dishes, wrappers, glasses, and even food out on the counter. Apparently, he thought that he was living in a luxury hotel with the privilege of having servants follow him around.

Mom decided to do an Academy with her son, but he was 6 feet tall and weighed 165 pounds. She knew that she couldn't put him in Time Out or hold him down, so she had to get his attention in a different manner.

Consulting with Bill, she worked out an appropriate strategy. As her strapping adolescent came in the door after school one day, she asked for his car keys. Once they were in her possession, she stated in a calm tone, "Robert, once again the kitchen was in a mess this morning. I realize that griping at you is annoying, so I won't do that anymore. What I realize by your actions is that I haven't trained you very well and you probably don't know exactly what to do."

As you'd expect, that set off an attitude and Robert responded that he'd handle the problem later. Fine, said Mom, but Robert would have to complete the Academy *before* he'd be allowed to eat dinner, and *before* he'd get his car keys back. Frustrated, Robert bolted out of the house. After 45 minutes, Robert returned and noisily began cleaning up his mess in the kitchen. Mom turned to him and remarked, "Robert, your practices don't count until they are done quietly and with a good attitude and under my supervision."

At that point, Robert yelled an expletive and retreated into his bedroom. Over the next day, he tried everything he could think of to get out of the Academy. He tried shifting his problem onto Mom, saying, "You know, you better give me my car keys, otherwise you have to take me to school, and I have to be there early tomorrow."

Mom, who had rehearsed a response, replied that she'd be happy to give him his car keys as soon as he practiced cleaning the kitchen to her liking. In the meantime, Robert would just have to figure out how to get to school on his own or take whatever consequence the school dished out.

After a few more blowups, Robert finally agreed to perform the Academy. And after a couple of false starts, he did exactly what Mom asked, six times—all with a good attitude.

Mom did not have to deal with a dirty kitchen again. She did, however, have to give Robert Academies for other problems, such as taking out the trash and cleaning up his room. While Robert's behavior wasn't perfect at home, the big difference was that Mom finally felt in control of her house, and she felt empowered.

One note here: We do not recommend withholding food when training younger children, only when you need more leverage when working with adolescents—as in Robert's case. For most younger children, Time Outs and Hold Downs will suffice.

Three Ways You Can Short-Circuit This Technique

In our practices, we have found that parents often make similar types of mistakes when they first try Academies. First, parents commonly expect an Academy to work magically after the first time. But think about it this way: Most of us didn't learn to ride a bike after one attempt, and children usually don't adopt good behavior after one intervention. Children require time, attention, and effort. Difficult children require even more of the same.

Defiant children usually require repeated Academies for a behavior. If your child has a developmental delay or is explosive and inflexible, he will probably need repeated exposure to Academies, which work extremely well with this type of child. And when children have a skill deficit, making them practice an appropriate behavior just once probably won't penetrate their memory banks. We have seen children require up to 15 Academies for a behavior before they get it down. As always, if you are seeing some progress, don't give up.

Another common problem is that parents feel that an Academy must immediately follow the misbehavior.

Wrong.

Most misbehavior happens because children are upset, angry, agitated, or overly distracted. The best time to have your child practice an Academy is when he is calmer and his emotions aren't paralyzing his thinking process. It can occur as much as several days later.

Remember, children are not like dogs. Children have a working memory and can recall what happened several days before. If you don't believe this, make your child a promise and see if he can recall it several days later. Dogs, on the other hand, must have a consequence immediately following the behavior. Otherwise, they don't associate their behavior with the consequence. You can't be training your dog to heel and only snap his choke chain 20 minutes after he failed to heel two blocks ago.

Your child, though, can put two and two together, even though you might have to give him a gentle reminder. So feel free to wait until both you and your child have chilled. That way, the Academy will more likely have a positive impact.

Another common problem occurs if parents give their children Academies when they are convenient for the children. The purpose of making an Academy inconvenient is to get your child's attention—to make it an ordeal for him and therefore motivate him to use the appropriate skill the next time.

One mother complained to Ray that Academies were not working for her son. After conversing with her further, Ray discovered that she

BEHAVIOR BASICS

The Keys to an Academy

1. How you say it is 90 percent of the battle. Use sadness in your voice and explain to your child that his behavior is telling you that he needs practice.
2. Have your child practice the behavior you want, repeatedly.
3. Have your child practice at a time that is convenient for you and, if possible, inconvenient for him.
4. If necessary, break the behaviors or procedures down into their smallest components.
5. Be patient. Learning and permanent behavior changes are gradual.

was having the boy practice speaking nicely to her (the Academy) while they were in the car going to hockey practice or running errands. Her son was a captive audience. What else was he going to be doing with that time? Looking out the window? The Academy wasn't having an impact because it did not inconvenience him, so it wasn't an ordeal.

Make sure that the Academy occurs when your child has something else pleasurable planned.

Academies are a consequence, not a punishment. If your child's behavior improves after one Academy, then you can stop the Academies. The purpose is not to make your child "hurt." You are trying to help the child master a skill or be more motivated to demonstrate that skill the next time it is required.

So what happens if your child totally refuses to do an Academy? Funny you should ask: That's our next point. You would tell the child that his behavior is telling you that he is not really in a thinking mood, and that he needs to go to Time Out to figure out whether he wants to cooperate.

Exercising the Future Muscle

Teaching Your Child about Choices and Accountability

Picture the brain as a network of muscles. Within that group is one particular strand that we'll call the Future Muscle. In your youngster's body, the Future Muscle, like most other muscles, is thin and has not been exercised much.

Most children do not spend much time thinking about the future. The types of children this book is written for—defiant ones—tend to spend even less. They are extremely impulsive. Their Here-and-Now muscles grow every day, but their Future Muscles remain largely ignored.

We often hear parents describe their defiant children by saying, "He's a delightful child, as long as he's doing what he wants to. The minute you ask him to do something else, he becomes a monster." That's an indication that his Here-and-Now muscles are in charge.

When he's thinking about whether he should do something, he

makes the decision based on the answer to this question: "Is this activity something that would give me pleasure now?" If the answer is no, he does something else. If it is yes, he gets into the cookie jar, uses your compact discs as Frisbees, or does whatever else will be fun right now.

A defiant child just thinks, "I'm going for it."

Building Mental Muscles

You may believe that your defiant child doesn't consider any of the consequences that his actions might bring, but give the child some credit. It's not that he isn't thinking; it's just that he isn't making good decisions. He is making a plan but not considering possible consequences for himself or other people.

So what can you do to change his approach? Combine some of the techniques we've mentioned elsewhere in the book to create opportunities that help him exercise his Future Muscle. Here are the steps.

1. Give your child choices whenever possible. For example, if he often causes trouble when it's time for a bath, ask him whether he'd prefer to take a bath in the upstairs or downstairs bathroom. Simple "kid choices" like this give him a sense of control, which he loves, and they help him practice making decisions. They also exercise his Future Muscle.

2. Catch your child in the act of behaving appropriately. If your goal is for him to not throw a basketball inside the house and you notice him throwing a Nerf ball instead, use an acknowledgment to let him know that you appreciate the improvement. It's important to comment on even slight improvements in behavior like this. Even if your child isn't doing the precise behavior you'd like to see in an ideal world, he is showing improvement and he needs to hear that you've noticed.

3. Don't warn your child of specific consequences before he misbehaves. He needs to learn that something will happen, even if

it's not spelled out in advance. This helps him start considering the future. Also, not knowing what the consequences will be forces him to think. So, if you tell your son not to throw his basketball inside the house and he does it anyway, don't warn him; just sadly tell him that he won't be going to basketball practice this week (a significant consequence). If it comes out of the blue this time, then next time he'll realize that you mean business and he'll pay more attention to the words that fall from your mouth.

4. When you give your child a consequence, offer it with sadness, not anger. For example, if he throws a fit when you tell him to clean up his toys, take a moment to compose yourself, and then emphasize how sad you are that his behavior has earned him a consequence. Responding this way keeps the struggle within the child and not between *you* and the child. You want your child's mental energy to be focused on solving the problem, not on getting angry at you.

5. Practice keeping the monkey on his back by using brain-dead phrases. Like using sadness in your voice, this makes your child angry at the consequence he has earned, not at you. It also helps you avoid getting into arguments. So, if he calls you "the rottenest mom in the world!," just say, "Sorry you feel that way," and walk away.

A Test Case

Bill once counseled a parent whose 8-year-old son, Gregory, was very impulsive. Gregory's 6-year-old brother had a tendency to get on Gregory's nerves, as little brothers often do. Gregory coped with his younger brother's annoying behavior by slugging the tiny brat in the head.

To prevent that reaction, Gregory's father began to implement the Future Muscle plan, and he made sure that the negative consequences were things that caught Gregory's attention. Foremost, the father let Gregory experience his own consequences. When

Gregory popped his brother with a right hook, the Future Muscle plan kicked in. Gregory was first placed in Time Out. He then had to do an Academy by reliving the situation and pretending that his brother was agitating him. Gregory then had to practice different and appropriate ways to deal with his brother, such as allowing his father to intervene, walking away, giving in to his little brother, and so on.

After several weeks of this program, the little brother annoyed Gregory one afternoon. Their father sat on the couch reading a newspaper, just feet away from where Gregory's left hand held his brother while Gregory's right hand was clenched into a fist. Suddenly, Gregory's Future Muscle flexed.

"Dad, will I get in trouble if I hit him?" Gregory asked.

His father replied with a simple, almost disinterested "Yup," and Gregory pondered his consequence for a moment. He then set his brother down and said "Darn!" without laying a hand on him. His thought process was: "Here's what I want to do at the present time, which is slug my little brother. Hold it. I understand. I remember the consequences, so I better do some more thinking. I don't like these consequences. Forget it. Let's do something different."

The Future Muscle's development added flexibility into Gregory's thinking. It's not that he would never get frustrated again. That is not normal. The point is not that Gregory's little brother would stop bugging him or that Gregory wouldn't want to hit him. The point is that Gregory had to find a different response—a different way of handling things. Thanks to his Future Muscle, he began solving his own problem.

Offer Positives as Well as Negatives

You need to give your child lots of choices and consequences so that he will be held accountable and begin using his Future Muscle. But it's important that you blend in positive and constructive consequences—not just negative ones. Providing both helps your child analyze the results of his actions.

When he receives a positive consequence, he starts to ask himself, "What didn't happen? I wasn't punished. I didn't have to spend my TV time doing an Academy. What did happen? I got to watch television (or play with my friends, or use the telephone, or use another privilege that is important to me)."

Of course, often, when you give your child choices, he is going to choose poorly and his misbehavior may result in an Academy. That is a negative consequence, but it is something that he needs to experience over and over again. Academies are one consequence that exer-

BEHAVIOR BASICS

Five Ways to Develop Your Child's Future Muscle

1. *Give your child choices whenever possible.* This gives him a sense of control and helps him practice making decisions.
2. *Catch him being good.* Comment on behaviors that you want to see more of, even if they aren't notably positive behaviors. Example: If your child is playing quietly in the living room, say, "I notice that you are playing quietly."
3. *Don't always warn your child of the specific consequences before he misbehaves.* All that children need to know is that something will happen. This creates an environment that enhances their future orientation. When your child knows that there will be some consequence to his misbehavior, he is forced to think ahead.
4. *When you have to offer a consequence, say it with sadness— not anger—in your voice.* This keeps the struggle within the child and not between you and the child. When consequences are given with anger, the child tends to battle with you.
5. *Practice keeping the monkey on his back.* Use brain-dead phrases. Here's an example.
   CHILD: *You're meaner to me than to Joey.*
   PARENT: *I'm sure it feels that way.*

cises children's thinking muscles, their abilities to reason, and their Future Muscles.

The next time your strong-willed son is about to misbehave, hopefully he will stop and think: "Hold it, hold it, hold it. I might have to go into Time Out and then do an Academy if I hurl Dad's Chicago CD. I don't like being in Time Out and I especially don't like doing those dumb Academies. Never mind."

That will encourage him to carefully place your compact disc in its case, grab a real Frisbee instead, and run outside to act on his desires in a manner that is positive for both him and you. (However, it should be noted that Ray thinks the *only* good use of a Chicago CD is as a Frisbee.)

Chapter 22

Parenting Miscues

Bag the Behavior Chart . . .
and Other Things That Don't Work

*I*n our more than 50 years of combined experience counseling parents and kids, we've seen or developed a number of effective ways to help defiant children change. (The best of the ideas are in this book.) But we've also run across strategies and attitudes that are ineffective or, worse, that do much more harm than good.

We're not saying that all these methods and attitudes are worthless in all applications—just that in our experience they don't work well, especially with defiant children.

In this chapter, we'll look at four of the most troubling of these issues and explain why we feel that each is unproductive.

The Bad Side of Behavior Charts

We know that many therapists and health care professionals will react with outrage when they hear this, but we strongly recommend that you either don't use behavior charts at all or else use them sparingly—for 6 weeks or less.

When Ray worked at Children's Hospital in Richmond, Virginia, he became quite the expert at designing behavior charts for kids. But after a short period of time—usually 3 to 6 weeks—those behavior charts would inevitably stop working.

Ray assumed that the parents were at fault for not carrying the plan through effectively. He figured that parents had stopped following the prescribed directions. This was partly true: Parents did get tired of using them because charts are inherently burdensome, meaning that it takes a lot of mental energy and time to monitor them. It also requires planning to constantly remember to carry along enough poker chips or stickers or whatever reward you're offering.

But the bigger problem is that children acclimate to these charts and stop working as hard to earn rewards. More important, while behavior charts can help some children learn new skills, they do not help kids maintain and continually use those skills. We have found that when you try to modify behavior only through the use of a behavior chart, the child readily returns to his old behavior routine as soon as you remove the chart or system.

Finally, behavior charts do not accurately depict the real world. How many people do you know who use a behavior chart at work? How often does your supervisor put a smiley-faced stamp on your chart? Under the best of conditions, most of us get a paycheck every 2 weeks. This is no behavior chart.

We are not saying never to use behavior charts or that they are always bad. For some kids, these charts are a good bridge. They help the kids get to the point where they can work under a more "real-life" plan, such as the one that this book offers. Also, charts can be a real lifesaver for children with conduct disorders who are in residential treatment centers, or for children with severe attention deficit hyperactivity disorder (ADHD).

However, behavior charts are not a long-term solution.

The Risk of Rewards

All too often, we have seen doomed behavior-chart programs in schools. One example is a system in which students get a point for every half-hour that they behave and concentrate on their tasks. After 5, 10, or 20 points, they earn a special privilege such as extra computer time or drinking a Coke with the principal. We psychologists call this an "if-then" procedure: If you behave, then you get a reward. There are a number of drawbacks to this strategy, the first being that the child tends to focus almost exclusively on the reward rather than on the importance of behaving.

Bill has a young stepson named Zach, whom the O'Hanlons were trying to teach an innovative method of playing the violin. Like most youngsters taking on a new project, Zach was pumped up at first but quickly lost steam. To reenergize him, Bill bought the boy some Matchbox play cars and told Zach that he would get one car for every 30 minutes that he practiced. The boy practiced, but he was eyeballing the Matchbox cars more than the paper music that he was supposed to be following. Before long, even the lure of the cars couldn't hold his interest.

Look at professional athletes these days. They aren't working any harder than athletes did 20 or 30 years ago, but they certainly are demanding more reward. Most don't play just for the fun of it anymore, do they? And you can probably see the same thing happening in your home. Many children who have been put on a reward program for behaving at school or for getting ready for school in the morning do one of two things after a few weeks. First, as time goes by, they want a larger reward for producing the same behavior. Second, they won't behave unless the program remains in place. In other words, they will not ever behave without the promise of earning a reward.

The second drawback is that by rewarding children for behaving the way they should, you risk damaging their internal motivation. While this is a controversial issue among experts in the field, we both have had many experiences in our practices that validate this notion. Several parents have told us about making a simple request of their child, only to have their cherub respond, "What are you going to do, pay me?"

Using Behavior Charts Short-Term

Again, we are not condemning all use of behavior charts. And we are not implying that all children should never receive tangible rewards. Rather, we recommend a few modifications to the "standard" behavior chart and to the "standard" method of rewarding children with tangibles.

If you are determined to use a chart; first plan to use it as a short-term motivator. Reduce the rewards gradually and remove the chart as quickly as possible. The reason that we recommend rapid removal is because we have seen the problems that a behavior chart can cause over time.

Ray recently helped out with a student with severe behavior problems. The kid had been on the same behavior chart for several years. When the teacher was asked how long she planned to keep the boy on it, she looked at Ray with surprise—as though she had never thought about removing it.

Because the chart had just become part of his day-to-day life, the boy had no motivation to get off of it—or to improve his behavior. The chart actually was handicapping him.

Here's another good way to alter the chart: If you are rewarding children with tangibles, we advise you never to use "if-then" scenarios, if that's possible. If you plan to reward your child for good, positive behavior, don't tell him about the strategy in advance; just give him an appropriate reward when he displays the behavior you desire. If you tell him your plan, then you'll be obligated to give a reward—that's an if-then situation.

Let's say that your child does a particularly good job on his chores one day and you decide to take him to lunch as a treat for working so hard. This is a reward that was not expected—it did not motivate the child to do the chores well, because he didn't know that there was any reward involved. Had you told him that he would go to McDonald's for doing a good job, this trip to the Golden Arches would have become an obligation.

In real life, the principal doesn't come to a teacher and say, "Look, if you do a good job this year, I will make sure that you are named Teacher of the Year and get a $1,000 bonus." Instead, the teacher works hard all year doing the best she can. At the end of the year, she may or may not get the award and bonus. Her attention all year was focused on her performance rather than the reward.

By giving rewards to your child as you see fit and without prior obligation, you cause him to focus on his performance rather than on a prize.

A Better Response

Our experience is that children, even the "explosive" or inflexible kind, respond well to positive interactions with the adults in their lives. And they alter their behavior best when parents have them do Academies to practice appropriate behaviors. We've found this combination extremely effective in helping ADHD, defiant, explosive, inflexible, and down-right difficult children. This two-pronged strategy is the backbone of this book, and it is what we are recommending that you try first.

One last note: It is all right to *occasionally* set up an if-then situa-tion. This once-in-a-while occurrence will not ruin your child. To say "If you get your homework done, we will all go out to McDonald's" does not destroy the child's motivation or your relationship with him. But doing it repeatedly probably means that problems are on the way.

"Do as I Say, Not as I Do"

Unfortunately, drugs and alcohol have done plenty to undercut the American family. While this is not a book about the problems of drugs and alcohol, we do want to caution you that abusing substances will create many inconsistencies in your home. One of these, of course, is in parenting. We have found that the best way to deal with this situation is for the parent with a problem to receive treatment first while leaving the child's behavior problems on the back burner. Without treatment, parents who struggle with drugs or alcohol will remain inconsistent and their children will easily rationalize their own misbehavior.

Recently, a mother brought her 15-year-old girl to Bill's office because the teenager was defying rules, violating curfew, and disre-specting her mother. Upon further investigation, the daughter told Bill that she wasn't the only one "violating curfew." When asked what she meant by this, she said that her mother often goes to bars at night, calls home, and says that she'll be home in 20 minutes. But frequently, the mother doesn't show up until 3 or 4 hours later.

This mother had difficulty seeing how her drinking problem gave her daughter authorization to model those same behaviors. Until the mother comes clean, acknowledges her alcoholism, and becomes a better role model, her daughter's defiance will likely continue.

Vagueness

Way too often, children get locked into the "land of vagueness" by their parents. That is, parents will not be specific enough with their children about what kind of behaviors they expect. For example, a parent will say, "I want to see a better attitude from you," or "I want you to be more responsible."

Your child may try to exhibit a better attitude and claim more responsibility, but his actions may not match what you had in mind because he doesn't know exactly what you have in mind. A child may try being kind to his brother during supper in an attempt to display a better attitude; however, you may also notice that he continues to talk back and roll his eyes at you. Later, he will try to negotiate more privileges because he feels that he has demonstrated a better attitude. You, on the other hand, say that his attitude remains poor because you've only observed the eye-rolling. Naturally, your child will feel discouraged and angry.

Vagueness allows a problem like this to materialize in the first place. You can avoid this pitfall by being specific in detailing the behaviors that you want to see. The best way to do this is to use what we call video examples to let your child know precisely what you expect. (See "Rewarding Small Changes" on pages 98–99 for more on video examples.)

Closing Down the Possibility for Change

Bill's mother used to tell him, "Be careful what you ask for, you may just get it." Over the years, we've found that you even have to be careful how you think about a situation, because you just may create it.

Many times, parents in therapy say, "He can't do such-and-such. He's ADHD [or fill in your child's diagnosis here]," or "He's just like his father."

If you make statements like these, you are closing down the possibility of change. The word *can't* means "never." Saying "He's like his father" means that the child is genetically predisposed to do something and that there can be no altering of the future.

BEHAVIOR BASICS

Four Techniques and Attitudes to Avoid

1. *Behavior charts.* Charts that reward kids for good behavior encourage kids to behave only when there is a prize involved. Take away the incentive and the child will likely return to his old ways.
2. *"Do as I say, not as I do."* You can't expect your child to change an inappropriate behavior if you exemplify that same behavior. He's much more likely to be influenced by your actions than by what you say.
3. *Vagueness.* If you're not clear about how you want your child to change his behavior, he can't respond in an appropriate way. So don't tell him, for instance, that he needs to improve his attitude. Spell out specifically the behavior that you want him to adopt.
4. *Closing down the possibility of change.* Making negative statements about your child—"He can't do such-and-such"—discourages him from changing. A better approach is to make statements that leave open possibilities. Example: "It is more difficult for my child to do this."

Though these statements may appear subtle, therapists have known for years that they dramatically influence our environment.

Your child interprets your statement as self-defining. When he hears something that he construes as negative, he thinks that you have given up on him, so he gives up on trying to change. You can overcome this problem just by slightly changing your wording. You may find it hard to believe that a word here or there can have much impact on your child, but it can. All you have to do is go from saying "My child can't do this," to saying "It is more difficult for my child to do this," or "He reminds me of his father, and in some ways he's different." This opens up possibilities.

United We Stand

Why Parents Must Take Complementary
Approaches to Raising a Defiant Child

*E*ddie's parents went through a bitter divorce but eventually moved to within a few blocks of one another for Eddie's sake. The child's father, Jim, had remarried soon after the divorce was final—a development that inflamed his ex-wife's anger. Eddie's mother, Rose, began telling Eddie how Jim and "that woman" had destroyed their family and that his father really didn't care about either of them.

When Eddie stayed at Jim's house 3 nights a week, he was sullen and uncooperative, occasionally escalating into defiance. He would refuse to do chores, and when told to do his homework, Eddie would claim that he was "too upset" from the divorce to focus on the work (even a year after the breakup). If Jim insisted that Eddie do as he was told, Eddie would throw tantrums and say that he hated his father, who had "destroyed my family."

Between visits, Eddie would play on his mother's sympathies. He told her how unfair Jim was being and how he hated to go over to his father's house. Rose eventually called Jim to tell him that Eddie really didn't feel comfortable at his house with "that woman." She suggested that perhaps they should take a break from visitations for a while until things calmed down. When Jim insisted that Eddie continue the court-ordered visitation agreement, Rose became angry and hung up the phone.

Unable to resolve this dispute their own, the couple ended up back in court—with Eddie caught in between.

Too often, defiance can be created or made worse when parents—married or divorced—put the child in the middle of their conflicts and use inconsistent approaches to discipline him. Parents do not have to have exactly the same approach or style of parenting, but it is important for them not to undermine each other and to at least have complementary approaches.

Every child needs consistency, but a defiant child needs it even more. When parents send a strong-willed child mixed signals, it just invites him to test limits and misbehave.

There are three key situations that promote mixed signals and defiance:

▸ Disagreements between married spouses over parenting styles
▸ Divorce and its repercussions
▸ Dating and remarriage

Let's look at ways to cope with each of these issues.

Parental Discord

One of the biggest and most common pitfalls in a child's development is parental discord between married spouses. This is where you and your spouse are openly (or even subtly) at war over how to discipline your child.

When a defiant child receives mixed messages about how to behave, it ends up reinforcing his misbehavior. The misbehavior may even worsen. If you and your spouse have reached this point in your home, you need to make some changes quickly.

We recommend that you ask your spouse to take a neutral position.

Let's say that you believe in Time Out while your spouse is an advocate of spanking. In order to give each of you a fair shake, you may say to your spouse, "I know that you don't buy this new approach, but would you please let me try an experiment for 2 months? Please don't undercut me, roll your eyes, or bad-mouth me [or anything else you may expect your spouse to do] while I'm experimenting with this new process. After 8 weeks, if our child hasn't improved at least a little, I will follow your plan for 8 weeks—without undercutting you—as long as your plan is not violent or illegal."

When your spouse assumes a neutral position, you are more likely to have the leverage you need to work successfully with your child. Change will not happen immediately, so neither you nor your spouse should anticipate major improvements in the first 4 weeks. But if you watch carefully, you should see small changes that should lead to bigger and better ones.

Also keep in mind that beyond its effect on your child, discord with your spouse over parenting may be a symptom of deeper problems. There may be difficulties within your marriage or individual psychological ailments. If you suspect that either may be the case, we encourage you to seek counseling from a professional. There is no stigma in seeking help anymore.

Divorce: A Different Challenge

We don't want to downplay the problems created by divorce, but the effect of different parenting styles and household rules on your defiant child is not necessarily one of them.

Naturally, it is detrimental for any child to hear one parent bad-mouth the other, a situation that commonly occurs after a marriage dissolves. A child considers himself a mix of his mother and father. If you bad-mouth your ex-spouse, your child can take it quite personally and perceive you as bad-mouthing a part of him.

That said, it is perfectly acceptable for a divorced parent to tell a child that she doesn't accept the parenting philosophy the other ex-spouse has established, and that the child will have to adhere to separate rules in each household.

Children can easily acclimate to more than one style of discipline. Many children do this every day—multiple times a day—while at school. With a lenient math teacher, kids in algebra may resemble screaming hyenas. The bell rings, and they move into the stricter English teacher's class. Within 5 minutes, they have transformed into model ladies and gentlemen.

Another example is the case of the Garnetts. When the couple divorced, Mrs. Garnett let Michael, her 3-year-old son, sleep in her bed. She felt guilty for what he'd gone through and thought that he needed reassurance to get to sleep now that his father was not in the house.

But when Michael stayed at his father's house, Mr. Garnett insisted that the boy sleep in his own bed. Initially, every night at the father's house was a struggle, with the child yelling, "Mommy doesn't make me sleep in my own bed! I hate you, Daddy! You're mean!" After many weeks, Michael learned to adapt to the different rules, and he finally accepted the fact that he would have to sleep in his own bed at his dad's house.

A year or so later, when his mother began to want privacy in her bedroom, she had to go through a similar struggle with Michael to get him to sleep in his own bed. But her challenge was far less difficult since Dad had already stood his ground on the issue.

Clearly, having different styles and rules does not automatically create long-term problems. Obviously, the more consistency there is between the two households, the better. But we don't want you to think that it is absolutely mandatory for both households to be carbon copies of each other.

The Message Bearer

There is another issue that *can* affect a child of divorced parents and lead the child to defiance. That's when the parents place the child in the position of being a message bearer between them. The parents use the child as a messenger because they aren't willing to communicate directly with each other by phone or in person.

Sometimes, one or both parents also will use the child to spy on the other. A mother may quiz her child to find out how her ex-husband is doing emotionally or whether he is in a new relationship. Or the father may try to find out what his ex-wife's new partner is like or what the state of her finances is.

When children are used this way, the pressure often builds inside them until they finally explode, rebelling against each parent for placing them in the messenger role. Or, rather than exploding all at once, a child may take advantage of being the messenger and make false claims against each parent as a way to gain some benefit for himself. For example, he may tell you, "Mom says you took all our money. You should buy me a new pair of jeans because we don't have any money." Or "Dad says I don't have to obey you because you are irresponsible and had an affair."

If you are struggling through a difficult time with your ex-spouse, spare your child from playing the messenger. Instead, if face-to-face or telephone contact is too volatile or unworkable, you and your ex-spouse should arrange a more direct means of communication, through faxes, e-mail, or a third party (a mediator, a trusted friend, your lawyers).

We also urge both of you to separate the emotional issues in the situation from the discipline and parenting issues. If your child is upset about the divorce, tell him that his anger is a separate issue that can be discussed later. But for the moment, the issue at hand is the issue at hand. So, if your son grows angry because you refuse to buy him a new video game and accuses you of taking all the money from your spouse, tell him that you'll talk about the divorce at another time. Right at that point, you need to focus on why he doesn't need another video game.

The Danger of Disneyland Dads (and Moms)

Sometimes, a parent who has been criticized by a former spouse tries to counter the criticism by either buying whatever the child wants or doing any activity that the child wants to do. This has been called the Disneyland Dad syndrome. Obviously, this can play into defiance.

Another form of this syndrome, more directly related to creating defiance, is the parent who has received such "bad press" from the exspouse that he or she chooses not to discipline the child for fear of further damaging their relationship. Unfortunately, this often makes the child unmanageable and more defiant. In fact, it can lead to the precise alienation that the parent fears.

We have found that the longer a parent ignores discipline issues, the harder it is to finally create limits and consequences. So, we recommend enforcing the household and family rules from day one following the divorce or separation.

The Challenge of Dating and Remarriage

As much as kids might say that they want the newest video games, clothing, or music, what they actually crave more than anything else is

BEHAVIOR BASICS

Three Ways Parents' Relationships Can Affect a Child

There are three situations between you and your spouse that can negatively affect your attempts to parent your child.

1. *Disagreements in parenting philosophies between married spouses.* When you and your spouse openly disagree about how to raise your child, it leaves the child confused and prone to defiance.
2. *Divorce and its aftermath.* Divorced parents don't have to raise their child by the same rules, but it's important that the spouses don't bad-mouth each other or try to use the child as a messenger to avoid direct communication with each other. Another potential problem for divorced parents is refusing to discipline a child out of fear of alienating him further. This just makes the child more unmanageable.
3. *Dating and remarriage.* Both of these events throw a child's emotional reality off-kilter and can trigger defiance. If your child has become defiant during one of these events, it's important to deal with it quickly. Otherwise, the defiance may escalate.

a secure reality. When their reality is challenged during emotionally turbulent events such as divorce and parents' dating and remarriage, it can lead to defiance.

If you are dealing with one of these events, you need to be especially careful not to let defiant behavior go unchallenged. Otherwise, you could face serious problems.

The noted psychiatrist Milton Erickson, M.D., wrote about an 8-year-old who lost control when his mother, a single parent, began dating. The mother was reluctant to correct his misbehavior during this time, and the boy grew more and more defiant as a result. Not knowing where the limits were was frightening to a child that age. He kept pushing and exploding until finally, when nobody could control him, he pushed the limits so far that he destroyed property at home and in the neighborhood.

Only after the mother intervened with discipline and Hold Downs did the child learn to control himself.

Later, the child thanked her for providing some limits.

With more and more divorce and separation, more stepfamilies, more blended families, and more single-parent households and other nontraditional families these days, the challenges of parenting can be great. But whatever your circumstances, if you follow the suggestions that we have offered in this book, you can make progress even in the most trying of circumstances.

Chapter 24

Send-Off

10 Commandments
for Parents

In this book, we have tried to give you the tools and encouragement you will need to create a good relationship with your challenging child. We've also tried to create a context for your child to develop good personal and social skills.

As we were finishing the book, another tragedy of schoolchildren being shot by one of their fellow students unfolded in the national news. (Sadly, you may not even be able to determine when we are writing this, because we are certain that this won't be the last of these terrible instances.) As we read and heard the news stories about the student accused in the shooting, we ached when we heard of his parents' struggle to find help and to find ways to deal with their son's growing unruliness and disobedience in a more effective manner.

The parents, it seemed, did all the standard things. They gave consequences and spent quality time with their child in attempts to prevent the boy's growing obsession with violence from going any further.

But that was not enough.

This book goes beyond those methods. It actively enlists your child's motivation to solve the problem, which is especially crucial when dealing with defiant kids. We would like to think that we are offering some tools and ideas that might (and we stress *might*) turn a situation around before it escalates to such a devastating level of violence. We hope that you take this feeling on our parts not as arrogance (we certainly don't have all the answers about parenting), but as a statement of our passion and commitment to helping parents and children. We have actually seen these methods defuse dangerous and frustrating situations and create relationships filled more with love and cooperation.

Finally, to help keep things in perspective, we leave you with this story.

There was once a man who gave a class on how to parent. He called it Ten Commandments for Parents, and parents, being insecure about their abilities, came from far and near to attend his class and learn how to be better parents. The class was great: clear, funny, and helpful. At that time, though, the instructor was not married and had no children. One day, he met the woman of his dreams, and in time they had a child. He kept teaching but soon retitled his class Five Suggestions for Parents. He and his wife were then blessed with another offspring. He renamed the class Three Tentative Hints for Parents. After they had twins, he stopped teaching the class altogether.

Our ultimate goal in this book is to remind you that *you* can parent your strong-willed child yourself. Trust your judgment and stand firm. Pay attention to the results that you are getting, and if something isn't working, change your approach—even if you're using a technique that we suggested. You and your child are worth the time and effort.

Good luck.

Resources

Have you ever reached a point with your child where you're so flustered that you don't know how to respond to his behavior? We all have. At times like that, it's helpful to have some strategies to fall back on. Here are some of the most common situations we've run across in our practices, along with several ways to approach them. First are three "decision trees" that show you the appropriate ways to respond to each of your child's likely actions (just follow the arrows to see what you should do). Next, you'll find scripts for shutting down arguments. Finally, there is a list of organizations and additional reading to help you in your parenting journey.

Responding to Defiance, Step by Step

Situation 1

Arguing: Your child incessantly argues with you, trying to get you to change your mind about allowing him a privilege.

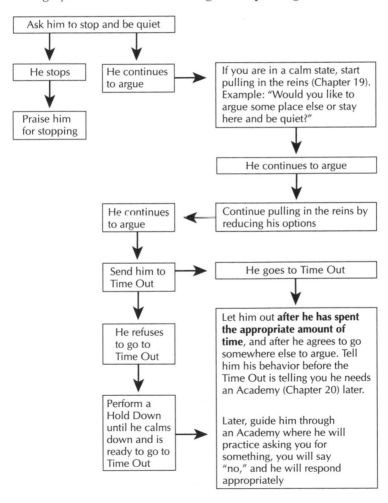

Situation 2

Noncompliance: You ask your child to do some task, such as clean his room. He puts you off ("I said I'd do it later"), and then never completes the task.

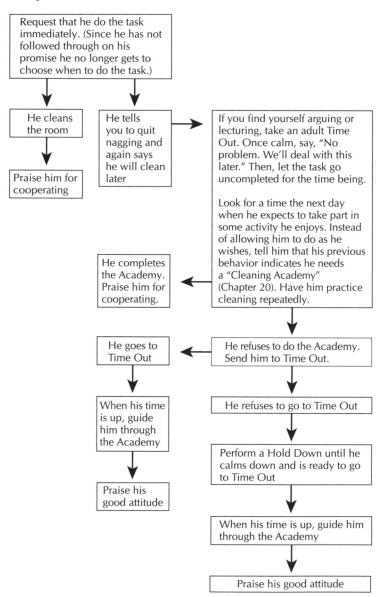

Situation 3

Aggression: Your child hits a younger sibling for some reason. Example: "He wouldn't play with me."

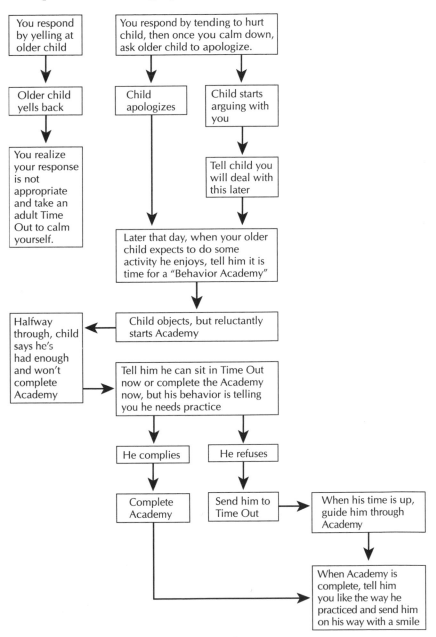

Scripts for Shutting Down Arguments

*D*efiant kids love to argue. They use arguing to postpone or talk you out of punishments, or even as a form of control: They know that if they can say something that gets you steamed, then they've got power over you, even if it's only for a moment.

Your best defense against these assaults is simple: Don't participate. Remember, it takes two to argue.

Easier said than done? Not really. You just need to take some simple steps to prepare yourself. First, you need to anticipate your child's arguments and figure out how to respond to them without losing your cool. That way, you won't be caught off guard when arguments come.

(In fact, anticipation is a good tactic to use in all interactions with your child. Parents of defiant kids generally expect the best from their kids, then get frustrated when they get the worst. If they just anticipated what was likely to happen, they not only wouldn't get frustrated, they'd be able to respond in a way that would help their kids learn.)

The second way you can cut off arguments when your child tries to get a verbal struggle going is to respond with Brain-Dead Phrases that shut off the debate. (See Chapter 9 for a full discussion of this technique.)

Here are several common situations and appropriate "scripts" you can use to respond appropriately to each one.

Scenario 1: Refusing to Clean Up after Himself

Your defiant child has developed a pattern of ignoring your commands or arguing with you over everything he is told to do. The situation comes to a head after dinner. He is watching TV with a sibling and you're getting ready to relax. Unfortunately, you can't because he's left a pile of toys around the house. You tell him it's time to clean them up so you can sit down without having to look at the mess.

CHILD: *It's not fair I have to miss my show.*
YOU (USING BRAIN-DEAD PHRASES STATED CALMLY): *You are probably right.*
CHILD: *Why do I have to clean up while Jenny can watch TV? She made the mess too.*
YOU: *You're probably right. I see a lot of your toys. Please pick them up now.*
CHILD (CONTINUING TO WATCH TV, BASICALLY IGNORING YOU): *OK.*
YOU: *Uh-oh! What you're telling me is you want me to solve this problem. I'll be happy to.*
CHILD (TRYING TO MAKE PARENT FEEL GUILTY): *I told you I'd do it. Why do you always have to be so mean and punishing?*
YOU (WITHOUT RESPONDING TO CHILD'S STATEMENT): *No problem, son, I'll solve it.*

End Result: You clean up the toys, while planning when you will later make your child complete a Cleaning Academy. (This Academy should take place during a time when he wants to do something else, such as go out and play with a friend.)

By responding in this way, you shut down the immediate argument and you give your child time to move from an emotional state to a thinking state. Remember, trying to get your child to comply when he is emotional is not as easy as gaining compliance when he is in the thinking state.

When he later completes the Cleaning Academy, he will learn that there are consequences for his procrastination and arguing.

Scenario 2: Drawing Comparisons to the Way You Discipline a Sibling

You have two children: one who is generally compliant and one who is defiant. The defiant child is continually fresh to you and he has been warned that he will face consequences if he talks this way to you again. During the course of a day, the generally compliant child makes a fresh remark to you. You scold that child and the child apologizes. Later, the defiant child does the same thing. And you impose a consequence:

CHILD: *That's not fair. When Sally was fresh you just yelled at her and let her get away with it.*
YOU (CALMLY): *Thanks for noticing.*
CHILD: *THAT SUCKS!! You got that out of that stupid book you are reading!*
YOU (ANOTHER BRAIN-DEAD PHRASE): *You're probably right.*

End Result: You continue to impose the consequence while refusing to respond to your child's attempts to make you angry and to distract you. If you shut down his attempts to argue, he has no choice but to obey or face greater consequences.

Scenario 3: Overaggressive Behavior

Your defiant child is overly aggressive and has been warned that hitting other people will result in a consequence. As you're watching, he "accidentally on purpose" runs into Timmy, the kid next door, knocking the kid's head into a wall. You institute a consequence by first sending him to Time Out.

CHILD: *It was an accident.*
YOU: (CALMLY): *Thanks for letting me know how you see it.*
CHILD: *But it's true!*
PARENT: *I don't believe you.*
CHILD: *But it was an accident. THAT'S NOT FAIR!*
YOU: *Sorry you feel that way. You can practice walking next to people respectfully later. Now you can go to Time Out.*

End Result: Again, you've shut down his attempts to argue and left him with no choice but to comply or face greater consequences. Note that you don't ask him to practice his behavior skills now. He needs to calm down first, and hopefully think about his behavior.

Scenario 4: Fresh Talk

You've agreed to give your defiant child and his friends a ride to the movies. Fifteen minutes before you're supposed to leave, your child is extremely fresh and rude to you. You tell him you can no longer provide a ride.

CHILD: *That's not fair; you promised.*

YOU (CALMLY): *I only do nice things for people who are nice to me.*

CHILD (TRYING TO MAKE YOU FEEL GUILTY): *If you back out now, you'll embarrass me in front of all my friends.*

YOU: *You're probably right.*

CHILD: *ALL RIGHT. I'M SORRY. Would you take me now?*

YOU: *Nice try. Ask me tomorrow; I'll probably have a change of heart.*

You then walk out of room. If the child tries to continue the argument, remain quiet and walk outside. Generally, defiant kids are afraid someone will see them acting inappropriately and will stop arguing if they're in public.

End Result: Leaving the room while continuing to refuse his request makes it clear that you're not going to change your mind, and that he needs to change his attitude to earn favors from you. You also let him know that you will not discuss anything when he is emotional, and that perfunctory apologies don't work for you.

Scenario 5: Inappropriate Dress

Your child, who has a problem of dressing inappropriately, comes down to breakfast wearing a tank top when it's 40 degrees outside.

YOU: *Do you think you're dressed warmly enough for the weather today?*

CHILD: *I'm fine, just lay off; you're such a control freak.*

YOU: *Glad I'm not the one who is going to be cold.*

You then back off.

End Result: Defiant children refuse to learn from your experiences so no amount of coaxing or complaining will change your child's mind. Instead, let him learn his lesson from the natural consequence of being cold when he heads outside.

Scenario 6: Refusing to Go to Bed

Your child refuses to go to bed on time and tries to extend his time with arguments such as: he was good all day, he didn't have his after-dinner snack yet, he didn't get to play the game you promised, etc.

CHILD (TRYING TO MAKE YOU FEEL GUILTY): *Pleeease! Can't I stay up just 10 minutes more? We didn't play checkers like you promised.*

YOU: *I know, Sweetie, but time slipped away. I can understand how disappointed you are.*

CHILD (TRYING TO DRAW COMPARISON WITH OLDER SISTER): *Jenny gets to stay up. That's not fair.*

YOU: *We've been over that many times. I imagine it will just feel unfair to you. Do you want me to read you a story or do you want to read to me tonight?*

End Result: By refusing to argue, staying calm, and offering your child choices that lead him toward your objective, you reduce the chances he'll continue to complain.

Scenario 7: Throwing Tantrums when He Doesn't Get His Way

Your child tends to throws a tantrum whenever you answer "no" to one of his requests, especially if he asks you to buy something when you are together in a store. This time you're in a toy store together when the tantrum starts.

CHILD: *I WANT THAT NEW COMPUTER GAME!*

YOU: *It's no fun going shopping with you when you act like this.*

CHILD (TRYING TO ENGAGE YOU IN A RIDICULOUS DISCUSSION IN THE STORE): *But you never buy me anything. You are so mean.*

YOU (WALK AWAY WITHOUT RESPONDING. LATER, WHEN BOTH OF YOU ARE CALM): *You know what your behavior in the store told me? You need practice accepting "no." So instead of going to the baseball card store now, we will sit here and we will practice hearing "no." I want you to ask me for various toys and games for 5 minutes and I will say "no" to each request. You are to practice handling that rejection appropriately. Don't worry about it, son, I'll be happy to practice with you until you are really good at handling "no." I love you that much.*

End Result: Walking away lets your child know that he cannot engage you in an argument during inappropriate times or places. It also lets him know that you will not even discuss the subject matter until he is calm and asks appropriately. Later requiring your child to do an

Academy built around accepting "no" shows him there are consequences when he throws a tantrum. Practicing appropriate responses over and over again helps him thoroughly learn correct ways to react when he doesn't get his way, thereby helping him develop better coping skills.

Scenario 8: Refusing to Do Homework

Your child has a problem with homework—he won't do it at all, does it sloppily, or refuses to apply any effort. When you tell him to do his homework, he responds rudely.

CHILD: *It's my work, my life. Leave me alone; this is none of your business.*
YOU (AS CALMLY AS POSSIBLE): *I know you feel that way, but my job is to make sure you are prepared to work in the adult world, and I'm not happy with the thought of your living with me at age 35. So I'll help you solve this problem.*
CHILD: *Just back off. I passed last year; I can do it again.*
YOU: *Probably so, but I've got a new plan. If your homework isn't done, you're telling me you need practice. I've asked your teachers to e-mail me every day with your assignments. If one assignment isn't done, I'll be happy to supervise your doing that missing assignment three to four times so you can practice doing it correctly. That goes for sloppy work too. Don't worry, I have plenty of time to help you after dinner and on the weekends.*
CHILD: *THIS SUCKS!*
YOU: *That's one way to look at it.*

You then turn and walk out of room, leaving your child until he regains control of himself and is back in the thinking stage. If he still refuses to do his homework or doesn't apply himself, you require him to complete the Homework Academy.

End Result: By calmly giving your child the choice of doing his homework rather than ordering him to do it, you let him have control, which he craves. You also make clear that if he fails to do his homework, he will be responsible for the consequence, which will be a much bigger ordeal than if he had completed it originally. However, expect to impose an Academy; these children most commonly learn by their experience, not by your warnings.

For Further Reference

Organizations
While there are no groups or associations directly linked solely to strong-willed children, there are several helpful resources that should be mentioned.

Children and Adults with Attention-Deficit/Hyperactivity Disorder (CHADD)
8181 Professional Place, Suite 201
Landover, MD 20785
(800) 233-4050
www.chadd.org

   This is a good resource for parents whose children have attention deficit hyperactivity disorder. The organization can direct you to support groups in your area as well as provide you with books from its catalogue on various parenting issues.

National Information Center for Children and Youth with Disabilities (NICHCY)
P.O. Box 1492
Washington, DC 20013
(800) 695-0285
www.nichcy.org

Federation of Families for Children's Mental Health
1101 King Street, Suite 420
Alexandria, VA 22314
(703) 684-7710
www.ffcmh.org

The Love and Logic Institute
2207 Jackson Street, Suite 102
Golden, CO 80401-2300
(800) 588-5644
www.loveandlogic.com

Jim Fay and Dr. Foster Cline have a catalogue of tapes and books that offer wonderful and simple advice about parenting and teaching.

Cates-Levy Consulting
17480 Dallas Parkway, Suite 230
Dallas, TX 75287
(972) 407-0808
www.cateslevy.com

Dr. Ray Levy and Joe Cates, M.Ed., do workshops together or separately on parenting and school issues. Additionally, they offer consultations for schools or school systems on discipline procedures and problems.

Books
Defiant Children by Russell A. Barkley (Guilford Press, 1987)

Parenting with Love and Logic by Foster Cline and Jim Fay (Pinion Press, 1990)

The Out-of-Sync Child: Recognizing and Coping with Sensory Integration Dysfunction by Carol Stock (Perigee Publishing, 1998)

A Field Guide to Possibility Land: Possibility Therapy Methods by William H. O'Hanlon and Sandy Beadle (Possibility Press, 1994)

Audio Tapes
Helicopters, Drill Sergeants, and Consultants: Parenting Styles and the Messages They Send by Jim Fay (Cline/Fay Institute, 1994)
Simple Solutions to Difficult Problems, a series of seven tapes available from Cates-Levy Consulting

Sources
The following books were used in the course of writing our book.

Taking Charge of ADHD: The Complete, Authoritative Guide for Parents by Russell A. Barkley (Guilford Press, 1995)
The Explosive Child: A New Approach for Understanding and Parenting Easily Frustrated, "Chronically Inflexible" Children by Ross W. Greene (HarperCollins, 1998)
The Hurried Child: Growing Up Too Fast Too Soon by David Elkind (Perseus Publishing, 1989)
Parenting by Heart by R. Taffel with M. Blau (Addison-Wesley, 1991)

Index

Underscored page references indicate boxed text. **Boldface** references indicate illustrations.

L

Lecturing, ineffectiveness of, 67–68
Listening
  for building relationship with child,
    90–91, <u>90</u>
  by child, Attending to Play for
    improving, 103–6, <u>104</u>
  selective, by children, 27

M

Manipulation
  brain-dead phrases for avoiding, 69,
    <u>70–71</u>, 72–73, 117
  as characteristic of defiant children,
    10–12, <u>14</u>
  examples of, 10–12, 69, <u>70–71</u>, 72
Medication, misbehavior and, 51–52
Misbehavior
  consequences for reversing
    logical consequences, 124, <u>130</u>
    natural consequences, 123–24,
      <u>130</u>
    vs. punishment, 121–23
    related consequences, 126–27,
      <u>130</u>
    relevant consequences, 125–26,
      <u>130</u>
    sequence for determining, 129,
      131
    significant consequences, 127–29,
      <u>130</u>
  Hold Downs for (see Hold Downs)
  medication and, 51–52
  signaling damaged relationship,
    86–87
  specific examples of
    aggression, 66, 100–101, 173–74,
      210
    challenging discipline, 209–10
    dinnertime problems, 49–50,
      72–73, 125–26, 127, 175–76
    fresh talk, 210–11
    inappropriate dress, 211
    manipulation, 10–12, 69, <u>70–71</u>, 72

morning battles, 3–6, 7, 24,
  115–16, 166–67, 169–70
noncompliance, 20–21, 74, 108–9,
  128–29
refusing to clean up, 18, 176–77,
  208–9
refusing to do homework, 128,
  164–65, 213
refusing to go to bed, 211–12
rudeness, 72–73, 175–76
school problems, 32, 51, 129
smoking, 126
temper tantrums, 10–12, 15–16, 20,
  35, 37, 117, 212–13
Time Outs for (see Time Outs)
Training Camp, steps for using
  do something different, 116–19,
    <u>118</u>
  pick a time, 115–16, <u>118</u>
  pick one misbehavior, 114–15,
    <u>118</u>
Morning battles
  Academies for, 166–67, 169–70
  examples of, 3–6, 7, 115–16, 166–67,
    169–70
  parental solution for, 24
  Training Camp for, 115–16
Motivation(s)
  blending positive and negative
    for changing defiance, 34–35,
      37–38
    for preparing for real world, <u>36</u>
  of children
    achievement, 9, <u>11</u>
    control, 9–10, <u>11</u>
    friendship, 9, <u>11</u>
  from desired experience or goal, <u>11</u>,
    35
  lack of, in defiant child, 66–67
  negative, in defiant children, 34
  positive methods of
    listening, <u>90</u>, 90–91
    positive attention, 84–87, <u>90</u>
    quantity time, 87–90, <u>90</u>
  positive vs. negative, in horse and
    camel analogy, 33–34
Myths, parenting, about defiant
    children, 47–52, <u>52</u>

PARENTS!
SHELF